CONFIDENTIAL

SUPREME HEADQUARTERS ALLIED EXPEDITIONARY FORCE
EVALUATION AND DISSEMINATION SECTION
G-2 (COUNTER INTELLIGENCE SUB-DIVISION)

B-A-S-I-C   H-A-N-D-B-O-O-K

KL's

(Konzentrationslager)

AXIS CONCENTRATION CAMPS AND DETENTION CENTRES

REPORTED AS SUCH IN EUROPE

The Naval & Military Press Ltd

Published by
The Naval & Military Press Ltd
Unit 10 Ridgewood Industrial Park,
Uckfield, East Sussex,
TN22 5QE England
Tel: +44 (0) 1825 749494
Fax: +44 (0) 1825 765701
www.naval-military-press.com
www.military-genealogy.com
www.militarymaproom.com

In reprinting in facsimile from the original, any imperfections are inevitably reproduced and the quality may fall short of modern type and cartographic standards.

T A B L E   O F   C O N T E N T S

		Page
1	General	1
2	Definition of Concentration Camps	2
3	Number of Camps and Inmates	3
4	Commitment and Release	3
5	Administration	4
6	Camp Organisation	5
7	Methods of Identification	7
8	Concentration Camp Guards	8
9	TV Regiments	8
10	TV Functions	9
11	TV Strength and Auxiliaries	10
12	TV War Service	10
13	Uniforms	11

ANNEXE A

LIST OF IDENTIFIED CONCENTRATION CAMPS

Key	A1

Part One: **Concentration Camps Grouped Territorially**

Baltic States	A3
Belgium	A3
Bulgaria	A3
Channel Islands	A3
Danzig	A3
Denmark	A3
France	A4
Germany:	
Baden	A5
Bayern	A5
Böhmen und Mähren	A5
Braunschweig	A6
Bremen	A6
Hamburg	A6
Hessen	A6
Mecklenburg	A6
Oldenburg	A6
Preussen (grouped by provinces: Brandenburg, Halle-Merseburg, Hannover, Hessen-Nassau, Holstein, Magdeburg, Magdeburg-Anhalt, Ost-Preussen, Pommern, Rheinland, Schlesien, Schleswig-Holstein, Westfalen, West-Preussen)	
Reichsgaue (Kärnten, Niederdonau, Oberdonau, RB Wien, Saarland, Steiermark, Sudetenland)	A8
Sachsen	A9
Thüringen	A9
Württemberg	A9
Greece	A10
Holland	A11

		Page
Part One (contd)	Hungary	A11
	Italy	A11
	Norway	A11
	Poland	A12
	Slovakia	A14
	Yugoslavia	A14
	Unlocated	A14
Part Two:	Alphabetical List of Concentration Camps, with Detail	A15
Part Three:	SS Arbeitsstäbe Not Located Near a Concentration Camp	A119

ANNEXE B

Diagram

THE GERMAN CONCENTRATION CAMPS

1. **General**

   This publication represents an attempt to compile the names, locations and pertinent data of confirmed, reported, or alleged detention centres in Axis Europe which come within the elastic definition of the term "Concentration Camp". "Elastic" because of the many types of detention camps used by the Germans in addition to the official Konzentrationslager (Concentration Camps). Among these are:-

   Arbeitslager (Work Camps)
   Zwangslager (Forcible Detention Camps)
   Zwangsarbeitslager (Penal Servitude Camps)
   Zivilgefangenenlager (Detention Camps for Civilians)
   Straflager (Punitive Camps).

   Recent political and military developments in Europe are said to have established new trends in German concentration camp policy, but these reports have not been adequately confirmed.

   Greater leniency towards inmates of concentration camps has been reported. A former inmate of ORANIENBURG said that the beating of inmates there has been forbidden and in SACHSENHAUSEN the guards are said to have been informed that the inmates should be treated as "property of the Führer".

   HITLER is stated to have intervened on behalf of the inmates at DACHAU. As a result, a brothel (?) is said to have been opened for the inmates, and permission was granted for the clearing of a soccer field.

   Other factors which might cause a change in policy include the deterioration of the guard system and the transfer of inmates to war time activities. One report expressed belief that, at the present time, the hatred of the SS men towards their commissioned officers is greater than that for the inmates.

   Various preparations made by camp officials have been reported in case of an Allied invasion of Germany proper. Stores of poison gas are said to be kept at some camps and inmates have been threatened that they would be shot or poisoned immediately upon the arrival of Allied troops. SS Officers are said to have civilian clothes hidden under their beds. For the camp at VUGHT, at least, it has been reported that the Commander intends to turn over the camp to inmates who are allegedly members of the former Communist Party of the Netherlands in order to create turmoil and prevent records and men from falling into Allied hands.

   It should be remembered that KL's, in addition to proving a social and political problem may also furnish a considerable number of Germans well disposed towards the Allies. Furthermore, KL's must be considered as potential sites for the detention of those Germans believed, suspected, or proved to be war criminals, or likely sources of disaffection at the time of the Allied occupation of Germany. Needless to say, these sites may also furnish quarters for the Allied occupational forces.

2. Definition of Concentration Camps

According to German law, a <u>Konzentrationslager</u> (officially abbreviated to KL, but popularly referred to as KZ) provides <u>Schutzhaft</u> (Protective Custody) for persons who have not been legally sentenced to prison by a court of law, and/or for those who, having served a legal sentence, have been ordered further detention by the <u>Gestapo</u> (Secret State Police), <u>Sicherheitsdienst</u> (SD or Security Service) or the <u>Geheime Feldpolizei</u> (Secret Field Police).

Because of the scarcity of documentary material, which is only slowly becoming available, the indefinite nature of details obtained from former inmates and the similarity in administration and treatment of charges at these various detention centres, many camps have been incorrectly reported as <u>Konzentrationslager</u> although they are actually different types of establishment.

Reports are often vague concerning the true status of many camps, being almost invariably incomplete, based on hearsay, mutilated in transmission, distorted in some fashion or out of date.

Legal definitions for the camps differ widely in the various German-occupied areas of Europe. For example, <u>Straflager</u> (Punitive Camps) in Poland are frequently somewhat similar to prisons, and serve the same purpose, but the treatment of inmates may correspond to that practised in concentration camps in Germany.

There appears to be no definite formula for the establishment of detention centres. New camps often are attached to existing penal institutions. A <u>Konzentrationslager</u> may be added to or use the facilities of a <u>Zuchthaus</u> (Penitentiary). An instance of the latter case was the use by the KL ORANIENBURG of the crematorium at the PLÖTZENSEE <u>Zuchthaus</u>. Concentration camps may be expanded by the addition of, for example, a <u>Straflager für Arbeitsverweigerer</u> (Penal Camp for Persons Refusing to Work).

PW <u>Dulags</u> (<u>Durchgangslager</u>, or Transit Camps) and internment camps have appeared erroneously in some lists as KL's, perhaps because the term <u>Dulag</u> may be applied also to collecting stations of all sorts for <u>Schutzhäftlinge</u> (Persons in Protective Custody). The <u>Dulags</u> mentioned in the list (Annexe A, Part Two) however, are most likely for <u>Schutzhäftlinge</u> and in no way connected with those of the armed forces of Germany; they deserve therefore to be incorporated.

Movements of inmates from one camp to another, especially from camps in occupied territory to those in the Reich have been reported rather frequently during the last two years.

Regular <u>Wehrmacht</u> penal establishments are referred to as SK's (<u>Soldatenkonzentrationslager</u>, or Soldiers' Concentration Camps) or <u>Sonder KZ's</u> (Special Purpose Concentration Camps).

3. Number of Camps and Inmates

Comprehensive reports on concentration camps, including estimates of the number of inmates in KL's, the number of camps in Germany and German-held areas and the number of men engaged in operating, administering and guarding these camps are not available as yet.

The number of KL's in greater Germany has been estimated at various times during 1941, 1942 and 1943 to total from about thirty to seventy-five, although a total of more than a hundred camp sites has been reported. The capacity of KL's in Germany is probably about 500,000.

A report, dated October, 1943, concerning the camps in Poland spoke of the existence of 109 camps in that country, divided into the following types:-

> Nine Transit Camps
> Twenty-four KL's
> Three large forced labour camps
> Sixty smaller forced labour camps
> Three camps for priests
> Nine camps for Jews
> One camp "for the improvement of the Nordic race".

Unconfirmed estimates have estimated the number of Germans who have been inmates at various periods during the years 1933 to 1944 to be between 750,000 and 1,300,000.

The most conservative estimate of the number of persons in "protective custody" in Germany proper in July, 1944 was from 170,000 to 370,000.

The number of KL inmates in Germany proper at present is generally estimated to total between 300,000 and 500,000. Of this number a high percentage is believed to consist of "pure" Germans, as defined by Nazi law.

In 1942 it was reported that SS men, in conversation among themselves, guessed the number of Germans then in "protective custody" to be about one million.

The number of inmates of these detention centres in Europe has probably been reduced as a result of Germany's man power shortage and many former inmates may already have been absorbed by the Organisation TODT and other labour and auxiliary organisations. Even the Wehrmacht has accounted for some - the 999th. Division for example.

4. Commitment and Release

The Einweisung in KL's (Commitment to Concentration Camps) may be effected by both branches of the Sicherheitspolizei (Sipo, or Security Police).

The Gestapo (both Amt IV of the Reichssicherheitshauptamt in Berlin and its branches and sub-branches) normally commits and may release those persons charged with, but not sentenced for, political offences and crimes. This is officially designated Schutzhaft (Protective Custody).

The Kriminalpolizei (Kripo or Criminal Police; both Amt V of the Reichssicherheitshauptamt and its branches and sub-branches) commit "BV's" (Berufsverbrecher or habitual criminals) and may (?) also release them.

As the various Leitstellen or Stellen (regional control HQ) of the Kripo are not necessarily organised along identical lines, the Inspektionen (Inspectorates) and subordinate Kommissariate responsible in each such HQ for committing persons to KL's do not always correspond.

5. Administration

German Concentration Camps are controlled by the SS Wirtschafts- und Verwaltungshauptamt (SS Economic and Administrative Department) and the Reichssicherheitshauptamt (Department of National Security, which is the head office of the Gestapo and the Security Service). Both these departments form part of the Reichsführung-SS (SS High Command).

The SS Wirtschafts- und Verwaltungshauptamt (abbreviated as WVHA) administers the camps, having complete control over all personnel, including the guards and prisoners.

One of the chief functions of this department is the supervision of the SS-Unternehmungen (SS Enterprises), for which prison labour is employed. Most camps use the labour of their inmates, and in some cases factories have even been built within the camps. The WVHA is in charge of the products of such work.

The Deutsche Ausrüstungswerke (DAW or German Equipment Works), one branch of which is located in ORANIENBURG, are said to have a main office in Berlin, and in liaison with WVHA take a share in the production activity of the camps.

The WVHA, whose Headquarters are in Berlin, is divided into several Amtsgruppen or branches. The branch which handles concentration camp matters is Amtsgruppe D, Führung und Verwaltung der Konzentrationslager (Command and Administration of Concentration Camps). Its offices are located at ORANIENBURG, twenty miles north of Berlin.

SS Obergruppenführer Oswald POHL is head of the Wirtschafts- und Verwaltungshauptamt and responsible to HIMMLER.

Amtsgruppenchef (Chief of Branch) of Amtsgruppe D is Richard GLÜCKS, who holds the ranks of Gruppenführer in the SS and of Lieutenant General in the Waffen-SS.

Formerly Stabschef (Chief of Staff) of the Totenkopfverbände, SS-Gruppenführer EICKE, who was killed in action on the Eastern Front in February, 1943, was the original Inspector of concentration camp guards (Inspekteur der Totenkopfverbände) and if this office still exists GLÜCKS may well have succeeded to it. There was, at least up to 1941, an official known as the Inspekteur der Konzentrationslager (Inspector of KL's), who was independent of Amtsgruppe D. No further information regarding the continued existence of this office is available, however.

The following Ämter (Departments) have been identified within Amtsgruppe D:

- Amt I   This Zentralamt (Central Department), which is headed by SS Obersturmbannführer Arthur LIEBEHENSCHEL, is responsible for general policy, security arrangements, public relations and co-ordination of the other departments within the Amtsgruppe.

- Amt II   Headed by SS Obersturmbannführer Gerhard MAURER, this department has charge of the general administration of prisoners.

- Amt III   The Medical Department, under SS Obersturmbannführer Dr. LOLLING, is responsible for general medical and health administration of all camp personnel, both staff and prisoners.

- Amt IV   This department supervises the general administration of camps and camp staffs.

Amtsgruppe C, (Bauwesen) another branch of the WVHA, controls works and buildings and, therefore, supervises the construction within the camps of plants of the DAW referred to previously. It directs the activities of concentration camp personnel who are drafted into SS Bau Brigaden and SS Bau Bataillone (SS Construction Brigades and Battalions) for employment on SS building and construction programmes or for clearing bombed areas.

6. Camp Organisation

Richard GLÜCKS as head of Amtsgruppe D is the Führer der Totenkopfverbände und Konzentrationslager (Commander of the Death's Head Formations and Commissioner of Concentration Camps).

While the methods of organisation and administration of camps differ in the various German-held sections of Europe, the following outline is believed to be fairly representative of the basic structure of such establishments.

The "great mystery" of the camps is the Politische Kommissar (Political Commissar). He is a Gestapo official from the Politische Abteilung (Political Section).

This section is subordinated to the Gestapo and/or the Sicherheitsdienst through Amt IV (Gestapo) and Amt VI (Sicherheitsdienst), both of which are part of the Reichssicherheitshauptamt (RSHA, or Department of National Security).

Regional control is exercised by the Gestapo through its Leitstellen and Stellen, and by the Sicherheitsdienst through its Leitabschnitte and Abschnitte.

In some respects the Political Commissar in a camp is the superior of the Lagerkommandant (Camp Commandant) and may even have the latter removed. Normally, however, he does not interfere with the administration of a camp, except in an emergency.

There may be several such commissars at one camp, but their names are generally unknown and they are seldom seen.

A Political Commissar receives double the pay of a Lagerkommandant and, in addition. RM 45 daily for a "travel allowance".

The rank of a <u>Lagerkommandant</u> is usually in accordance with the importance and size of the camp of which he is in charge. He works closely with the Political Commissar, and is jointly responsible with the latter for the conduct of the camp, but in addition he is responsible for the safety of the camp.

The camp guards are under the command of their own officers, but the latter execute the orders of the camp Commandant in so far as such duties as posting of guards and sentries are concerned.

As deputies, the Commandant has one or more <u>Lagerführer</u> (Camp Sub-commanders), the number depending upon the size of the camp; they generally hold the rank of <u>SS Untersturmführer</u> (2 Lt.), and function as section leaders.

Another post, about which little is known, is that of <u>Rapportführer</u>, who calls the roll at all parades, and probably comes under command of the <u>Lagerführer</u>. <u>Rapportführer</u> exist in most camps, certainly in the larger ones.

Under the Commandant, as adjutant and general supervisor, is the <u>Hauptwachtmeister</u> (Chief Warden), a post often filled by the CO of the SS men. He controls the <u>Platzmeister</u> (Wardens) who have charge of working parties.

Under each <u>Lagerführer</u>, as his NCO, is an <u>Arbeitsdienstführer</u> (Works Supervisor), who is in direct contact with the inmates and keeps a record of the work to be performed by them.

Assisting the <u>Arbeitsdienstführer</u> (Works Supervisor) are <u>Vorarbeiter</u> (Foremen) and <u>Arbeitskapos</u> (Labour or Works Bosses). These foremen and overseers are usually chosen from among those prisoners who are serving court sentences for common crimes and who were committed to the camps by the Criminal Police rather than by the Secret State Police.

In some camps they are graded and known as <u>Kapos</u> or <u>Capos</u> (Bosses), <u>Ober-Kapos</u> (Superior Bosses) and <u>Haupt-Kapos</u> (Chief Bosses). These superiors may either wear an arm band with the inscription <u>Kapo</u> on the left upper arm or <u>Gefreiterwinkel</u> (stripes similar to those of a German corporal).

In charge of the living quarters in the camps are <u>Blockführer</u> (Block Leaders). Poorly paid, these officials supplement their incomes through bribes and similar means, though, of course, they are not the only camp officials to do so.

Prisoner parties which work outside the camps, under the supervision of a <u>Kommandoführer</u> are known as <u>Kommandos</u>. There are usually two guards for every five prisoners, and every third guard is armed with a submachine gun.

Among the inmates the <u>Lagerältester</u> (Camp Senior Inmate) is believed to hold the most privileged position. His duties are not clear but reports indicate that he receives his orders from the <u>Lagerführer</u>, and in some instances, he has even been reported to be the "right hand man" of the <u>Lagerkommandant</u>.

Ranking below the foregoing officials are the <u>Blockältester</u>, who may be compared with an Army First Sergeant; the <u>Blockschreiber</u>, who is comparable to a Company Clerk, and the <u>Stubenälteste</u> (Room Wardens), who are prisoners in charge of rooms.

In general, it may be said that all persons holding the title of <u>Führer</u> are SS men and all the <u>Ältesten</u> are inmates. Like the foremen, the <u>Ältesten</u> are frequently habitual criminals.

Political inmates are said to have been entrusted with such jobs since they often wielded great influence over their comrades; but as they refused to commit cruelties and preferred torture to denouncing anybody they often lost their positions.

The Ältesten seem to be free of all other camp duties.

Ordinarily there are two doctors in each camp, one attending to the SS personnel and the other to the inmates. The nurses or medical assistants are largely recruited from among the inmates.

It is noteworthy that many clerical positions within the camps are held by inmates, some reports telling of a comparatively high degree of prisoner self-administration. According to one report, an attempt was made to run the camps with SS personnel exclusively, but the plan failed because there was too much graft, bribery and pilfering.

Employment of camp inmates for office work, which very few of the SS men could deal with efficiently, provides the camp officials with an opportunity to "play" the inmates against one another and to make them the scapegoats for thefts and other petty crimes committed by the SS men.

7. Methods of Identification

Inmates in most KL's wear colour patches, indicating the reason for their detention; these are usually on the right breast, but may also appear on the trouser leg. Since all camps do not have the same types of inmates, these patches vary accordingly. Local conditions and orders of the individual commandants also are responsible for variations in the size, shape or colour of the patches.

The following list shows the patches which appear to be most generally used. Wherever other types have been reported they have been noted in Annexe A, Part Two under the camp in question.

(1) Red — Politische Verbrecher (Political Criminals)

(2) Pink — Sexualverbrecher (Sex Criminals) Colloquially "175 er"

(3) Green — Kriminalverbrecher (Common Criminals); generally the only legally sentenced inmates.

(4) Brown — Arbeitsscheue (Those unwilling to work) mostly Gypsies.

(5) Light Blue — Gewohnheitsverbrecher (Habitual Criminals)

(6) Purple — Bibelforscher und Pazifisten (Religious Criminals and Pacifists; those opposed for religious reasons to Nazism, e.g., Jehovah's Witnesses)

(7) Yellow — Jews usually wear a yellow triangle with a red one superimposed, the two forming a six-pointed star; often, however, only the yellow Star of David, bordered in red, is used.

(8) Black   A black border around the yellow triangle worn by Jews denotes "Rassen schande" (Race Pollution). A six-pointed red star outlined in black also has been reported as denoting these inmates.

Colour patches numbered above 1 to 6 are usually equilateral triangles, about five inches in height, pointing upward. A black letter in a triangle, especially in the case of a political offender, denotes the latter's nationality, e.g. N for Norway or P for Poland.

One report described a red triangular patch, pointing downward, in the centre of which, in black, was the inscription SAW (Sonderaktion Wehrmacht, or Special Action, Armed Forces).

Inmates are also distinguished by having their hair cut short, or their heads partially or entirely shaved.

8. Concentration Camp Guards

The guarding of the concentration camps was entrusted originally to a special branch of the SS recruited in 1933 from volunteers of the Allgemeine SS and known as the SS Totenkopfverbände (TV or Death's Head units, so called because they wear a skull and crossbones on the right collar patch of their uniforms). But wartime demands on German manpower have diverted many of these ruthless troops to other tasks, and they have been replaced by older SS men, both German and foreign.

All Allgemeine SS and Waffen SS personnel wear the skull and crossbones on their visor caps, but the emblem as a collar patch has been reserved for the TV since 1935. Originally it was the flag emblem of all SS forces. (The Death's Head of the TV must not be confused with that of German tank personnel, from which it differs in that the TV skull has a jaw bone)

The first concentration camp at DACHAU, Bavaria, was opened officially on 18 MARCH 1933. The first 150 TV men were selected on 17 March, 1933.

Volunteers for the TV signed up for twelve years, all of which were considered as military service. They were paid in accordance with Wehrmacht schedules. The men receive military training and were organised as motorised infantry along the same general lines as the other full-time militarised units of the SS (the SS Verfügungstruppen, or General Service Troops) formed at the time.

9. TV Regiments

The Totenkopfverbände were originally organised into four Standarten, named after the areas in which they served, as follows:-

OBERBAYERN, original home station at Dachau, near Munich;
BRANDENBURG, original home station at Sachsenhausen,
   near Berlin;
THÜRINGEN, original home station at Buchenwald, near
   Weimar;
OSTMARK, most of the personnel of this regiment were
   recruited from among Austrian SS members.

Units bearing the name of "Elbe", "Sachsen", "Oranienburg" and "Ostfriesland" have been mentioned since about 1938, but these names may designate Sturmbanne (Stubas, or Battalions) or sub-units of Standarten rather than regiments.

These four regiments were placed under the command of the late SS Gruppenführer EICKE as Inspector and subsequently Commander of Concentration Camps and Totenkopf units. Previously he had been commandant of the Oranienburg camps. EICKE was killed on the Eastern Front in February, 1943.

Each Standarte was divided into Sturmbanne (battalions), designated by Roman numerals, and these battalions into Hundertschaften (companies), which consisted of 80 to 120 men or more, according to requirements.

The strength of such a TV Standarte was generally greater than that of a regiment in the Army. In 1936, for example, a report on Standarte BRANDENBURG stated that it consisted apparently of six Sturmbanne numbered I to VI, with Hundertschaften numbered consecutively from 1 to 24. Gaps in the company series may have existed, however.

Each Hundertschaft was organised and armed like an ordinary rifle company in the Regular Army.

It was planned originally that the unit to be stationed at a concentration camp should be a Sturmbann, but in practice the actual size of the unit depends upon the size of the camp concerned.

10. **TV Functions**

TV units are also organised along functional lines as follows:-

> Streifendienst u. Rollkommandos Patrols and raiding pursuit squads, e.g., detachments searching for escaping prisoners. In occupied countries HJ-Roll-kommandos or HJ Jagdkommandos are mentioned as auxiliary raiding squads and pursuit detachments under the command of SS-TV officers. These units are said to be composed of 15 to 16-year-old recruits from the Hitler Youth Organisation who have not yet entered into the German Labour Service.
>
> Wachverbände Guard Formations
>
> Sonder-Verbände (S-Verb.) Special Purpose units. These are reported to furnish execution squads, often operating in areas distant from their home stations.

11. TV Strength and Auxiliaries

Prior to 1939 the TV were said to number 25,000 officers and men. The highest (unconfirmed) estimate in 1939 was 40,000.

Successive levies of men for the field formations of the Waffen SS have left the original Totenkopfverbände considerably reduced both in numbers and in quality. As a result, there was an influx into the TV of foreign volunteers, who, though they are in no way below standard in brutality towards prisoners, do not have the same political loyalty to the Nazi regime. A large number of these foreigners in the concentration camp guards are Volksdeutsche ("racial" Germans) from the Balkans. But because of the needs of the fighting front, these men are often elderly, physically defective or otherwise unfit for active service.

SA Auxiliary guards, Werkschutz (Factory Police) and even Tartars and released Ukrainian PW's have recently been reported as concentration camp personnel, indicating the growing manpower shortage among the ranks of the TV.

It is also worth mentioning that TV personnel are not infrequently transferred from one camp to another.

S-Verbände are frequently referred to by the Roman numeral of the Sturmbann which controls them (e.g., S-Verband I under Stuba I).

An S-Verband appears to be organised often into Sonderkommandos der Totenkopfverbände (S-Kdo. d. TV, or Special Detachments). S-Kdo LAUSITZ and S-Kdo SACHSEN have been identified.

T-Einsatzstaffeln z.b.V (Death's Head Detachments for special assignments) have also been reported, and may be yet smaller units.

In addition there seem to exist E-Stürme (Ersatz Stürme, or Reserve Companies) quartered in some of Germany's larger cities. They bear the name of the town or city district in which their barracks are located, e.g., E-Sturm HAVEL.

SS TV-Verstärkungen (Reinforcement Units) have also been reported.

Among the service branches of the Death's Head Formations are the TV-Motordienst (Motorised Service), the TV-Nachrichtendienst (Signals Service), the TV-Sanitätswesen (Medical Service) and the TV-Ausbildung (Training Cadre).

12. TV War Service

The original function of the Totenkopfverbände was to guard concentration camps. But it was clear from the outset that HIMMLER also envisaged this picked force as one of his most effective instruments for repression within Germany in the event of unrest or insurrection. The combination of physical fitness, military organisation and concentration camp training made them eminently suitable for ruthless action, even against the German population. TV personnel are definitely known to have undergone on various occasions "training" to render them capable of unprintable cruelties.

In 1937 HIMMLER asserted that 3,500 Death's Head men guarded, as he claimed, 8,000 inmates of concentration camps. He explained that this large number of guards was needed as "no duty is so nerve-racking and fatiguing as that of guarding criminals".

The war has not yet provided an opportunity for any wide-scale repressive action by the Totenkopfverbände; at the same time it has seriously depleted the strength of these formations.

As early as the campaign in Poland in 1939 regiments drawn from the Totenkopfverbände fought along with the SS Verfügungstruppen as part of Germany's forces in the field.

In the winter of 1939-1940 an SS Totenkopf Division was formed from the first three of these combat regiments (now SS Pz Div Totenkopf). These Totenkopf field formations must be distinguished from the Totenkopf Standarten and Sturmbanne - which remained behind in their original capacity as concentration camp guards. The latter are frequently referred to as T-Wachverbände (Death's Head Guard Formations).

After the outbreak of war, the general term Waffen SS (Armed SS) was introduced to cover both the Verfügungstruppen and the Totenkopfstandarten. The Waffen SS though a branch of the SS is not in the official employment of the Nazi Party but is a specially regulated service of the Reich modelled after the Wehrmacht.

By an order issued in June, 1939, the finances of the Waffen SS were placed under the control of the Reich Minister of Finance and its property under the Minister of the Interior.

Thus the Waffen SS, including the Totenkopfverbände, is, in effect, a fourth arm of the service alongside the Army, Luftwaffe and Navy and its expenses are a State charge.

13. Uniforms

Men and officers of the SS-TV may wear the regular black uniform of the Allgemeine-SS or the field grey of the Waffen-SS, but show the skull and crossbones rather than the SS-rune on the right collar patch. Those who belong to the reserve formations wear grey instead of black collar patches.

The Waffenfarbe (distinguishing colour of the epaulette piping) for the TV is light brown.

Late in 1942 many concentration camp guard units were reported to have adopted the field grey tunics and trousers of the Waffen-SS because the civilian population near their camps considered them shirkers from combat when they appeared in their black uniforms.

Officers of the SS-TV may wear on special gala occasions a light grey uniform similar to that worn by the Sicherheitsdienst (SD). Because of this, the Totenkopf guards are referred to frequently as the "White SS", in contrast to the "Black" or Allgemeine SS.

The first TV Regiment (OBERBAYERN) wears as a special insignia the SS skull and crossbones superimposed on a narrow armlet to be worn on the left lower arm. Its members also seem to wear a death's head on both the left and right collar patches.

ANNEXE A

(List of Identified Concentration Camps)

KEY:

1. Annexe A gives all locations reported by various sources as sites of KLs at one time or another; such a list cannot of course be regarded as either complete or entirely reliable.

Of the 708 entries, 93 are cross-references.

2. Camps have been listed regardless of whether they are known to be still operating or whether they only operated in the past; thus camps in territory from which the Germans have been driven out are included, as information on past activities of persons connected with KLs is likely to be valuable.

Only rarely have the Germans closed camps in territory they still controlled, though the status of a camp has sometimes been changed, or its operation temporarily suspended.

PART ONE: LIST OF CONCENTRATION CAMPS GROUPED TERRITORIALLY.

3. Part Three gives an alphabetical list of camps in each country, the countries themselves being also in alphabetical order, as follows:-

Baltic States	Greece
Belgium	Holland
Bulgaria	Hungary
Channel Isles	Italy
Danzig	Norway
Denmark	Poland
France	Slovakia
Germany	Yugoslavia

Cross-references which occur later in the detailed list (Part Two), are given also in Part One.

4. "GERMANY": Germany, as explained under that heading, has been broken down territorially.

5. Territorial Boundaries: September, 1939 has been taken as the deciding date for frontier lines. Thus all camps in "Wartheland" are listed under "Poland", while the old Austria, Saarland and Sudetenland are found under the subdivision "Reichsgaue" in the "GERMANY" list.

Note, however, that the Prussian Provinces are given according to their most recent organisation.

PART TWO: ALPHABETICAL LIST OF CONCENTRATION CAMPS, WITH DETAILS.

6. Part Two lists all the camps alphabetically, with alternative foreign names in brackets, and the territory also in

brackets. Part Two contains all the information known about each camp.

7. **Details of Camps**: Dates of identification, inmates, type of camp, and personalities are given, also notes on the location of the camp.

SS units and establishments, which are frequently located near KLs, are also given.

8. **Dates of Information**: Wherever possible dates of reports are given, and may cover a protracted period. It is not always possible to ascertain whether the camp was actually in operation during the whole period.

9. **Personalities**: It has been difficult to obtain names, ranks, functions and dates of personalities connected with the camps, and contradictory reports have been received in some cases.

It is unlikely, however, that such personalities have been transferred to other duties, whatever change of function or camp may have occurred. This applies particularly to NCOs.

10. **Terminology**: Names and designations are given in the spelling and language in which they were reported.

It has not always been practical to translate units, and reference should be made both to the text and to other publications for ranks and abbreviations.

PART THREE:

11. Part Three is a list of SS Arbeitsstäbe (Works Control Staffs) not located near, or known to be connected with any identified concentration camps.

ANNEXE A

PART ONE

LIST OF CONCENTRATION CAMPS
GROUPED TERRITORIALLY

BALTIC STATES

Goldfials	(Unlocated)	Pleskau	(Northern Russia)
Kretynga	(Lithuania)	Proweniszki	(Lithuania)
Ostland	(Latvia)	Riga	(Lithuania)
Petrasiula	(Lithuania)	Viliampole	(Lithuania)

BELGIUM

From a general survey of Belgian concentration camps it appears that about one third of the camps were under Gestapo control, and it is from these that most of the transfers of inmates to camps in Holland are said to have been effected.

Twelve camps have been reported at one time or another in Belgium.

Achel	Jabbecke
Breedene	Lokeren
Breendonck	Malines
Hasselt	Schaerbake
Hoboken	Tervueren
Huy	Yvoir

BULGARIA

Ksanjije	Varna
Sveta Anestasia	

CHANNEL ISLANDS

Alderney	Sylt (See Alderney)
Jersey	

DANZIG

Danzig	Gdansk (See Danzig)
Danzig, District	Hela
Danzig-Matzkau	Stutthof

DENMARK

Elsinore	Frøslev
Farevejle	Horserød

FRANCE

A total of 78 camps, said to be KL's are reported as having been in operation at one time or another in France including Alsace-Lorraine.

Alliers	Miranda
Arc-et-Sonains	Mont-de-Marsan
Argeles-sur-Mer	Natzweiler
Arras	Nexon
Aubagne	Noe
Barreaux	Orleans
Bayonne	Paris
Beaune-la-Rolande	Pau
Belfort	Petite Roguette (See Paris)
Bouguenais	Pichey
Brens	Pithiviers
Charleville-Mezieres	Poitiers
Chauvailles	Pontivy
Compiegne	Recebedou
Doullens	Rieucros
Drancy	Rivesaltes
Dun-sur-Avon	Rouille
Ecrouves	St. Cyprien
Frejus	St. Etienne
Fresnes	St. Germain les Belles
Gaillin	St. Nazaire
Grasse	St. Paul D'Eyjaux
Gurs	St. Paul les Eaux
Hazebrouck	St. Privas
Jargeau	St. Quentin
La Lande a Monts	St. Renan
Lande	St. Sulpice-la-Pointe
Landerneau	Schirmeck
Larzac	Schmeker
Les Alliers	Sennheim
Les Milles	Sisteron
Le Verdon	Strassburg
Le Vernet	Toulouse
Limoges	Vals-les-Bains
Loissons	Vannes
Macau	Vesoul
Manzac	Vichy
Marseille	Vidauban
Mauzac	Vincennes
Merignac	Vorbruck (See Schirmeck)
Metz	Voves
	Watten

GERMANY

Of the 229 entries for Germany, 36 represent cross references. This does not imply that Germany has 186 camps, since all camps are not continuously in operation, and the same camp may have been reported under its correct name, the name of the nearest town or railway station, or the name of a region etc.

Illegible or garbled reports may account for different names for the same camp (e.g. Dürrheim or Dürkheim) but it seems safe to say that there are well over 100 camp sites in Germany capable of accommodating over half a million inmates.

The camps in Germany have been grouped for convenience into regional divisions, i.e. Länder and Reichsgaue, the latter being listed together under that heading and subdivided. PREUSSEN has also been subdivided into Provinces.

Baden

Ankenbuck
Bad Dürrheim
Baden-Baden
Heuberg
Käfertal
Karlsruhe
Kislau
Mannheim (See Käfertal)
Rastatt
Singen

Bayern

Ansbach
Bad Dürkheim
Bayreuth
Bernau
Bischofsgrün
Dachau
Dürkheim (See Bad Dürkheim)
Eila
Fechenbach
Flossenbürg
Frankenthal
Gotteszell
Hof
Kochel
Landsberg
Laufen
Lichtenburg
Limburg
Neustadt
Schirmitz
Stadelheim
Wasserburg
Würzburg

Böhmen und Mähren

Bilin
Breschan
Brezany (See Breschan)
Brünn
Klety
Lipnik
Mährisch-Ostrau
  (Moravska-Ostrawa)
Milowice (See Milowitz)
Milowitz
Pilsen
Plzen (See Pilsen)
Spielberg
Stepanov
Swatoborschitz, Kyjov
Terezin (See Theresienstadt)
Theresienstadt

GERMANY (contd.)

Braunschweig

Wolfenbüttel

Bremen

Bremen

Hamburg

Barmbeck
  (See Hamburg-Barmbeck)
Bergedorf (See Hamburg)
Fuhlsbüttel (See Hamburg)
Hamburg
Hamburg-Barmbeck
Neuengamme (See Hamburg)
Wittmoor (See Hamburg)

Hessen

Foehenheim
Ginsheim
Ginzheim
Griesheimersland
Grossenrohrheim
Langen
Obenrode
Osthofen

Mecklenburg

Aschenburg
Fürstenberg
Fürstenburg
Niederhagen
Ravensbrück
Rickling
Strelitz

Oldenburg

Ortumsand
Vechta

Preussen

a) **Province Brandenburg**

Alt Daber
Berlin
Bernau
Börnicke
Bötzow
Braetz-Schwiebus
Brandenburg
Jüterbog
Königswusterhausen
Lichtenfelde
Meinsdorf
Neurrandenburg
  (See Königswusterhausen)
Olympisches Dorf
Oranienburg
  (See Sachsenhausen)
Sachsenhausen
Schneidemühl
Senftenberg
Soldin
Sonnenburg
Uckermark

b) **Province Halle-Merseburg**

Erfurt
Gräfenhainichen
Torgau

GERMANY, Preussen (contd.)

c) Province Hannover

Arbeitsdorf-
  Fallersleben
Aschendorfermoor
  (See Emsland)
Berenbostel
Bergen Belsen
Börgermoor (See Emsland)
Brual-Rhede (See Emsland)
Burg Hoheneck
Dörpen, Walchum
  (See Emsland)
Emsland
Esterwegen (See Emsland)
Fallersleben
  (See Arbeitsdorf)
Farge
Harpstedt
Hastedt
Hoheneck
  (See Burg Hoheneck)
Krondorf (See Emsland)
Lager No. 21
Langluetjen
Lathen (See Emsland)
Moorlager (See Emsland)
Moringen
Neusustrum (See Emsland)
Oberlangen (See Emsland)
Osnabrück
Papenburg (See Emsland)
Watenstedt (See Emsland)

d) Province Hessen-Nassau

Kassel
Kassel-Melsungen
Melsungen
  (See Kassel-Melsungen)
Rödelheim
Sahra
Wetzlar
Wilsede

e) Province Holstein

Rendsburg

f) Province Magdeburg

Griebo

g) Province Magdeburg-Anhalt

Bernburg
Dornburg
Rosslau

h) Province Ost-Preussen

Braunsberg
Elbing
Dzialdowo (See Soldau)
Grundaus
Heilsberg
Labiau
Soldau
Tolkemit

j) Province Pommern

Hammerstein
Hohenbrück
Kolberg
Stettin
Vulkan Werft (See Stettin)

GERMANY, Preussen (contd.)

k) Province Rheinland

- Benninghausen
- Beyenburg
- Braunweiler
- Brauweiler
- Düren
- Hinzert
- Holbeckshof
- Jülich
- Kalkturm
- Kemna
- Koblenz-Karmelita
- Koblenz-Karthause
- Mühlheim
- Siegburg
- Wittlich (See Kalkturm)
- Wuppertal

l) Province Schlesien

- Frankenstein
- Gleiwitz
- Grossrosen
- Hoyerswerda
- Leschwitz
- Liebau
- Münsterberg
- Neubersdorf (See Nieborowitz)
- Nieborowitz
- Reichenbach (?)
- Waldenburg

Unlocated camp

m) Province Schleswig-Holstein

- Ahrensboek
- Eutin
- Glückstadt
- Heide
- Kiel
- Kolding

n) Province Westfalen

- Bergkamen
- Bochum VI
- Eilpe
- Sennelager
- Wanne-Eikel
- Wattenscheid

o) Province West-Preussen

Unlocated camp

Reichsgaue

a) Kärnten

Klagenfurt

b) Niederdonau

- Trützdorf (See Wöllersdorf-Trützdorf)
- Wöllersdorf-Trützdorf

c) Oberdonau

- Bretstein
- Gusen (See Mauthausen)
- Mauthausen
- St. Georgen (See Mauthausen)

GERMANY (contd.)

Reichsgaue (contd.)

d) RB Wien

Schwechat Wien-Schwechat
  (See Wien-Schwechat)

e) Saarland

Lerchenflur Saarlauten

f) Steiermark

Bruck/Mur

g) Sudetenland

Fischern Troppau
Opawa (See Troppau)

Sachsen

Bautzen Hohnstein
Burg Hohnstein   (See Burg Hohnstein)
Colditz Königstein
Crimmitschau Lichtenburg
Gräfenhainichen Mathilden-Schlösschen
Grünhainichen Ortenstein
Hainewalde Osterstein (?)
Hainichen Reichenbach
  (See Grünhainichen) Sachsenburg
  Zörbig

Thüringen

Bad Sulza Osterstein (?)
Blankenhain Untermassfeld
Buchenwald Weimar
Ohrdruf

Württemberg

Buchau Welzheim
Kuhberg

A9

GREECE

In some cases it is difficult to differentiate between prisons and concentration camps, as the Greeks had various open-air agricultural prisons and labour camps before the occupation. In a list of prisons in Greece 8 agricultural prisons and labour camps were mentioned.

Before the war the Greek method of dealing with political prisoners was to banish them to the Islands, but even so prisons in Greece were said to be inadequate for even the normal peace time incidence of crime.

There have been no concentration or internment camps in the true sense of the word since 1922, but after the occupation the Germans and Italians established them all over the country.

Agia
Agios Myron (Heraklion)
Alexandrouplos
Aliartos
Athens
Averoff
Chios
Corfu
Corinth (See Korinth)
Crete
Dhomokos
Didostxdion
Didymotikhon
Domokos
Edessa (Edessis)
Eleusis
Embirikos Asylium
Florina
Ghoudi (Goudi)
Hadjikosta Orphanage
Haidari
Halkida (See Khalkis)
Hios
Ipisti
Kallithea
Khaidari
Khalkis
Khios
Kirzali
Komotini
Korinth
Lamias (See Lianoklsdhi)
Larissa
Levadhis (Levadia)

Lianoklsdhi (Lianocladi)
Myros Iraklion
  (See Agios Myron)
Mytilene
Nauplia
Naxos
Palvos Melss
Paroi
Patras
Paulo Melas
Pavlou Mela Thessalonika
  (See Salonika)
Paxoi
Plannina
Salonika
Samos
Skolis (See Salonika)
Somovit
Syngrou
Tatoi (Tatoy)
Thebes (Thive)
Thive (See Thebes)
Tithorea
Trikkala
Tripolis
Tsikala
Volos
Voulgiameni
Vuria (?) Piraeus
Xanthi
Yeryeri (Amariou)
  Rethymnos
Ypati
Zanti

HOLLAND

Thirty camps were reported as KL's or similar detention centres in operation in the Netherlands at one time or another.

Almelo	Miechelsgestel
Amersfoort	(See St. Miechelsgestel)
Amsterdam	Moerdijk
Am Suhrskamp	Ommen
Arnhem	Oudleusden
Barneveld	St. Miechelsgestel
Blaricum	Scheveningen
Domburg	Schiedam
Ellecom	Schoorl
Gonda	Sluis
Haaren	Utrecht
Haren	Valkenburg
Heeren	Veenhuizen
Heilvareenbeck	Vught
Hertogenbosch	Westerbork
Hoben	Wierden-Almelo

HUNGARY

Szarvas

ITALY

Mantua	Rab

NORWAY

A general report on concentration camps speaks of "ten main camps", surmises a number of secondary ones and claims that any prison may be used as a transit camp for **Schutzhäftlinge** (persons in protective custody).

A total of 8,000 Norwegians were estimated to be detained in KL's of which Grini is said to contain one third.

A very recent report, however, claims that 4,000 Norwegian KL inmates were sent to Germany to work.

Twenty-nine camps are reported.

Berg	Kvam
Bogan	Lenes
Bollan	Nordmo
Brettvedt	Østerdalen
Dombaas	Oslo
Eggemøn	Saetermøn
Ekne	Seines
Espeland	Sem
Falstadt	Setesdal
Grini	Stavern
Hedmark District	Svanwik
Jernvaten	Sydspissen
Jörstadmoen	Tuesdestrand
Krokebergsleita	Ulven
Kvaenhangen	Verdalsøren

POLAND

Of the 192 entries for Poland 43 represent cross references, mostly the result of the fact that many locations are known by Polish as well as German names. The list includes camps in Poland as of 1st September, 1939.

Augustow I
Augustow II
Augustow III
Auschwitz
Belzec
Bendzin (See Bentschen)
Bentschen
Bialystok
Birkenau
Birnbaum
Bischofshofen
Bochnia
Bodzentin
Bogumin (See Oderberg)
Bohumin (See Oderberg)
Bojanow
Bomiechowek I
Bomiechowek II
Bozanowo
Bromberg
Brzezinki (See Birkenau)
Budzyn
Bukowa (See Kielce)
Cerwica
Chelm
Chelmno (See Kulm)
Chludow
Chojnice (See Konitz)
Chrubiesszow
Ciechanow (See Zichenau)
Czestochawa
   (See Tschenstochau)
Dabrowa
Debica
Dobrzyka
Drewnica
Dyle
Dziesiata
Dzezinka
Fort VIIa (See Posen)
Freistadt
Friedenshütte
Frydrychowka (See Lemberg)
Frystat (See Freistadt)
Garczyn
Garwolin
Glowna
Golcza
Gorczin

Görnau
Gorna Grupa
   (See Obergruppe)
Gorzyce
Grajewo
Graudenz
Grczyn
Grudziadz (See Graudenz
   and Obergruppe)
Helenow
Helm
Helmnok-Debia Estate
Hohensalza
Hrubieszow
Huta Beldon (See Beldon
   Hütte under Bentschen)
Huta Zgoda (See Friedenshütte)
Inowroclaw (See Hohensalza)
Jablonow
Jaslo
Jaworznia (See Kielce)
Jaworzyn
Jaworzyna
Jezierna
Kambinowski, Region
Kattowitz (Kattowice)
Kasmierz-Biskupi
   (See Bischofshofen)
Kielbasin
Kielce
Königshütte
Koldyrzewo
Konitz (Chownice)
Konstantinow
Konstantyn I
Kosminek
Kosow Podlaski
Krakau
Krasnik
Kulm (Chelmno)
Kutno
Lemberg (Lwow)
Leslau (Wloclawek)
Liban Quarry
Litzmannstadt
Lodz (See Litzmannstadt)
Lond
Lopuszno
Lublin

POLAND (contd.)

Lukow area
Lwow (See Lemberg)
Lyska
Majdanek
Malkinia
Maloszyce
Miechow
Miedniewice
Miedzychod (See Birnbaum)
Mlociny
Myslowice
Nakel (See Potulitz)
Nasielsk
Obergruppe (Gorna Grupa)
Obra
Oderberg
Ostrow
Oswiecim (See Auschwitz)
Pabianitz (Pabianice)
Pelninia
Piekoszow (See Kielce)
Pionki
Plasow (See Krakau)
Pleschen
Pleszew (See Pleschen)
Ploehnen
Plonsk (See Ploehnen)
Plock (See Schröttersburg)
Pomiechowek
Pomiechowek I
Pomiechowek II
Poniatow
Posen (Poznan)
Posen-Treskau
Potulice (See Potulitz)
Potulitz
Poznan (See Posen)
Preussisch Stargard
Przedzielnica
Puck (See Putzig)
Puszczykow (Pustkow)
Putzig
Radogoszcz
Radom
Radziwiliszki
Radzymin
Rajsko
Raua Ruska
Rembertow
Rippin

Rudniki
Rybnik
Rykosz (See Kielce)
Rypin (See Rippin)
Sapiezyska
Schröttersburg
Schwetz
Sichelberg
Sierpc (See Sichelberg)
Skalbmierz
Skarzysko
Smukla
Sobibor
Solec
Sosnowiec
Starachowice
Starogard (See Preussisch
   Stargard)
Swiecie (See Schwetz)
Swientochlowitz
  (Swientochlowice)
Swiety Krzyz
Szebunia
Tarnow
Tczew
Thorn (Torun)
Tomaszow
Torun (See Thorn)
Trawniki
Treblinka
Treskau (See Posen-Treskau)
Tschenstochau
Vilna (See Wilno)
Warschau
Wauer
Wielrenia (See Kielce)
Wilga
Wilno
Winnica
Wloclawec (See Leslau)
Wronki
Wysokie Brzegi
Zabikowo
Zacisze
Zakrzowek
Zamarte
Zambrow
Zamosk
Zascanki
Zascienek
Zgierz (See Görnau)
Zichenau
Zwierzyniec

SLOVAKIA

Bojnice   Chalmova

YUGOSLAVIA

Bacska Topola   Krapje
Bar (Bocche di Cataro)   Marburg/Drau
Begrade   Michendorf
Belgrade   Nish
Bocche di Cataro (See Bar) Sajmiste (Zemun)
Dedinje   Sarvar
Djakovo   Stara Gradiska
Ferincance   (Stare Gradiste)
Jasenovac   Velika-Kanija
Kosovska Mitrovica   Zagreb

UNLOCATED

Glasmoor   Three camps without
Karasjok   further definition
Zwringen

ANNEXE A

PART TWO: ALPHABETICAL LIST OF CONCENTRATION CAMPS, WITH DETAILS.

ACHEL
   (Belgium)
            The camp at HUY was reported to have been moved here.

AGIA
   (Greece)
            Near Khanoa, Crete; reported as KL.

AGIOS MYRON
   (HERAKLION)
     (Greece)
            Crete; reported as KL.

AHRENSBOECK
   (Schleswig-Holstein)
             Near EUTIN; last reported in 1936.

ALDERNEY
   (Channel Islands)
            "Sylt Camp" reported in February, 1944 to have 900 "political inmates". OT document addressed to Bauleitung "Adolf" (code name for ALDERNEY) refers to "KZ" Häftlinge in Feb 1944.

ALIARTOS
   (Greece)
            Attika Boeotia; KL established by the Italians and still reported functioning in June 43.

ALEXANDROUPOLOS
   (Greece)
            Western Thrace; KL established by Bulgarians; capacity unknown.

ALLIERS
   (France)
            Not confirmed; probably identical with LES ALLIERS (which would be the more correct name).
            See LES ALLIERS.

ALMELO
   (Holland)
            Only a Huis van Bewaring (Penitentiary). 60 reported there; see WIERDEN-ALMELO.

ALT DABER
   (Brandenburg)
            Near WUSTERHAUSEN; last reported in 1936.

AMERSFOORT
   (Holland)
            Type
               Dulag (Durchgangslager) with small KL annexe, which may be the camp for Jews in OUDLEUSDEN.
            Capacity
               Said to be 10,000.
            Inmates.
               In August 1943, 600-700 inmates were reported. They were prominent Dutchmen,

A

AMERSFOORT (Contd.)   members of the Orange Wacht, hostages, etc.
In March, 1944 reported numbers had risen 4,140, 3,000 of whom were to be taken to Germany by April 15th, 1,500 to the airfield RHEINE, and 1,500 to the airfield DÜSSELDORF. They were to remain prisoners guarded by the "Grüne" Polizei.
Guards
100 SS men (probably Dutch, and a few SD men.
SS Troops in the vicinity
An SS guard battalion of 400 men stationed there is said not to be connected with the camp. Elements of SS Panzer Division "Wiking and V./SS Artillerie Ausbildung und Ersatz Regiment (SS Artillery Training and Replacement Regiment) are also stationed in the vicinity. SS Wachbatl. 3.
Personalities
The camp doctor and NSB man KLOMP is the only personality reported.

AMSTERDAM (Holland)
Type
2 "Houses of Detention" reported. I at WETERINGSCHANZ and II at AMSTELVEEN-SCHWEG. Actually status is undetermined.
Capacity
Approximately 1,100 inmates reported in each prison.
Guards
Dutch, strengthened by a few SD men, who are subordinate to the SD at Euterpe Street, Inner Girl's High School (Commander, SBF LAGES).

AM SUHRSKAMP (Holland)
Near RATZEBURG; last reported 1936.

ANKENBUCK (Baden)
Reported 1936; not confirmed.
Reported 1943 as PW camp.
SS Guard.

ANSBACH (Bayern)
40 Km. SW NÜRNBERG.
Reported in July, 1942 as KL. May be identical with LICHTENBURG.

ARBEITSDORF-FALLERSLEBEN (Hannover)
Believed to be in operation. May only be a work camp.
Volks-werke (Volkswagen, People's car plant) in vicinity of ARBEITSDORF.

ARC-ET-SONAINS
(France, Doubs)

January, 1943, 190 Gypsies were reported there.

ARGELES-SUR-MER
(France, Pyrenees Orientales)

April, 1943, reported as camp for Jews and aliens.
Used to be an internment camp for Spanish loyalist soldiers.

ARNHEM
(Holland)

Type
A "temporary detention House" with 30-40 political prisoners under Gestapo control was reported here in August 1943.
SS Troops in the vicinity
The SS Panzer Grenadier Ausbildungs und Ersatz Btl. 12 (SS Panzer Grenadier Training and Replacement Btn. 12) is located near Arnhem.
SS Unterführerschule.

ARRAS
(France, Nord)

A camp for "political" internees and black marketeers reported in Aug 1943 at Rue des Carabiniers d'Artois.

ASCHENBURG
(Mecklenburg)

Reported in July, 1942.
Supposed to be for women only.
Also reported near WEIMAR.

ASCHENDORFER MOOR

See EMSLAND.

ATHENS
(Greece)

Pireaus Street, ATHENS; Hadjikosta Orphanage reported as KL with 200 inmates in Jan 44.
Reported also as the main gaol used by the Rallis Security Battalions to house hostages.
Said to have been condemned by Swiss Red Cross but is still in use.
For other camps in ATHENS Area see also GHOUDI and HAIDARI.
SS und Polizei Gericht Athens.

AUBAGNE
(France, Bouches du Rhone)

Marseilles region; no details reported.

AUGUSTOW I
(NE Poland)

Reported as civilian "Dulag".

AUGUSTOW II
(Poland)

30 Km. S. SUWALKI (SUDAUEN)
Reported as KL.

AUGUSTOW III   Reported as special KL with enclosures for women.

AUSCHWITZ (OSWIECIM)
(Oberschlesien, formerly Poland)

30 Km. SSE KATTOWITZ.
Type
Definitely KL: mentioned frequently since 1939. One report claims MAJDANEC to be part of Doppellager AUSCHWITZ.
BIRKENAU camp is definitely connected, as AUSCHWITZ makes use of BIRKENAU's gas chambers, though it is said to have 10 crematoria and 4 lethal gas chambers itself.
Capacity
In 1940: 40,000
A recent report claims 62,000 Jews and foreign workers to be employed in the synthetic rubber plant and other enterprises around this town.
Inmates
One report gives the following figures as an outline of the camp's history:
1939/40 - Over 5,000 inmates
July 1941 - 8,000 inmates, all Poles
Mortality rate 20% for each 6 month period.
Late 1941 - 600 Russians and 200 Poles gassed.
September 1942 - More than 120,000 persons had passed through the camp. Mortality has risen as over 80,000 are said to have died or been shot.
May 1943 - "At least 2 trains of 20 car loads each arrived daily".
1944 - Another report states that 150,000 names were listed as having passed through this camp.
Guards
6/SS Sturmbann KL AUSCHWITZ has been identified and may be a death's Head unit. One member, upon enlistment into the Waffen-SS served in this unit prior to his despatch to the Eastern Front.
Remarks
Many typhus epidemics are said to have raged here throughout its existence.
In the neighbourhood, reported to be at DWORY, is an I.G. Farben plant for synthetic rubber and "benzine", whose workers also live in nearby camps; slackers (those who take more than 2 days off per month) are confined to an Arbeitserziehungslager (Workers' educational camp) connected with the KL.
BUNA-WERKE (Synthetic Rubber Plant) draws labour from the KL.
SS Units in the Vicinity
Hauptwirtschaftslager der Waffen SS.

AUSCHWITZ (contd.)	Personalities		
	Rudolf HOESS	OSBF	probably commandant
	RÖDL	OSBF	Also reported as commandant (formerly Natzweiler)
	AUMEIER	HSF	deputy commandant
	BURGEN	SBF	
	Dr. Joachim CAESAR	SF	
	Dr. Edward WIRTHS	HSF	Garrison M.O.
	Dr. Kurt UHLENBROCK	HSF	
	Richard BAUR	HSF	
	Armand LANGERMANN	HSF	
	Fritz HARTENSTEIN	SBF	
	Emil STOCKER	HSF	
	Dec 1943		
	ZIEMESEN	HSF	Chief of camp administration
	v. BODMANN	OSF	
	SCHWARZ	HSF	
	SELL	USF	
	SCHOPPE	Uschaf	
	STIBITZ	"	
	MANDL		Senior wardress, formerly Ravensbrück Wardress
	Mar 1944		
	DRECHSLER		
	GRABNER	USF	
	VOZNITZA	USF	
	KIRSCHNER	(	
	BOGER	(Oschaf	
	LACHMAN	(	
AVEROFF (Greece)	Reported as prison, but may well be a KL.		

B

BACSKA TOPOLA (Yugoslavia)
KL reported there.

BAD DÜRKHEIM (Bayern)
Not confirmed.

BAD DÜRRHEIM (Baden)
Near Villingen.
Last reported April, 1938.
Possibly identical with BAD DÜRKHEIM.

BAD SUIZA (Thüringen)
Near WEIMAR
Possibly is not a KL, nor in operation at present.
In January 1943, "Russian Prisoners" reported there.

BADEN-BADEN
Not confirmed as KL.
Hauptwirtschaftslager der Waffen-SS in BADEN-BADEN

BAR (BOCCHE DI CATARO) (Yugoslavia)
Croatia.
KL under Italian and Ustashi control.

BARMBECK
See HAMBURG-BARMBECK

BARNEVELD (Holland)
A camp for "distinguished Jews" reported there in February, 1943.

BARREAUX (France)
Known as Fort BARREAUX (Isere).
Type
  Not confirmed as German or Vichy operated KL. May be a detention camp of another type.
Inmates
  July, 1943: 800 "escaped criminals" and Jewish black marketeers reported there.

BAUTZEN (Sachsen)
May be a Zuchthaus (penitentiary).
Last reported May, 1938.

BAYONNE (France, Basses-Pyrenees)
Inmates
  April, 1943: 200 French "communists" reported at the Citadel, doing forced labour.
  October, 1943: French hostages were reported as being sometimes transferred from the German controlled VILLA CHAGRIN to the Citadel.
Guards
  French and Belgian volunteer guards.

BAYREUTH
    (Bayern)

Not confirmed as KL.
A camp with 400 inmates was last reported here in 1936.

BEAUNE-LA-ROLANDE
    (France, Loriet)

Moved to DRANCY in July, 1943.

BEGRADE
    (Yugoslavia)

Location
    Not identified; probably an error for BELGRADE (q.v.).
Type
    "Special camp for Jews".
    A KL for all Jews from BELGRADE and vicinity.
Remarks
    Reported discontinued at the end of 1942, when the inmates were either shot or deported.

BELFORT
    (France, Alsace)

Status not determined. De Gaullists said to be held in the Fortress of BELFORT. August, 1940: the Friedrich Prison was reported to contain over 500 inmates.

BELGRADE
    (Yugoslavia)

Consists of 4 camps:-

(1) Gestapo KL "DEDINJE" reported there. 3,000 to 3,500 inmates. Commandant is named VUJKOVIC.

(2) 5, Aleksandrova Street; a Gestapo transit prison, generally between four and five hundred inmates; they stay usually over a month. Commander of the prison - NCO Johann RICHTER.

(3) KL "SAJMISTE": capacity 10,000. Inmates were at first Jewish families and later mainly Servian elements caught in mountains and woods. Overflow was sent to camp AEMUN. Direction of camp was under Ustashi control.

(4) Type
    Transit KL "ZEMUN".
Capacity
    Reported to be 80,000.
Remarks
    Is used to accommodate the overflow from camp "SAJMIST"

See also BEGRADE

SS Units in the Vicinity
    SS Pferdepark.

BELZEC
(Poland)
Location
   80 Km. NW of LEMBERG.
Type
   KL. Extermination camp for Jews.
Capacity
   10,000 Jewish inmates reported there.

BENNINGHAUSEN
Near BURSCHEID.
Last reported in 1936.

BENTSCHEN (BENDZIN)
(Poland)
Location
   12 Km. NE of KATTOWITZ.
Type
   Partly KL, partly Straflager for Arbeitsverweigerer (those refusing to work) in the KATTOWITZ mining region.
Inmates
   KL inmates have clean-shaven heads. Arbeitsverweigerer are allowed "short haircuts".
   1942: 21,000 Jews, Poles, Czechs and Ukrainians reported there.
Remarks
   A similar Straflager exists near the Beldon Hütte, (Huta Beldon), S IMMINENZ.

BERENBOSTEL
(Hannover)
Location
   Near HANNOVER.
Type
   The 25,000 inmates and SS Guards reported there in January, 1944, indicate a KL, but only a single source mentions this extremely large camp.

BERG
(Norway)
Location
   Near TØNSBERG
Guards
   Under control of "Quisling" police
Inmates
   October, 1942: 330 Jews are said to have been transported there from Germany. Aryan inmates remained there.
   November, 1943: some "students" were transferred there from BREDTVEDT.
   January, 1944: estimate of number of inmates was 300-500, including political prisoners.

BERGEDORF
See HAMBURG

<u>BERGEN BELSEN</u> (Hannover)	Near CELLE KL for Jews reported there in February, 1944. Bekleidungsamt der Waffen-SS in BERGEN BELSEN
<u>BERGKAMEN</u> (Westfalen)	Last reported May, 1938. Also reported as Work Camp for <u>Ost Arbeiter</u>.
<u>BERLIN</u> (Brandenburg)	COLUMBIA-HAUS Reported in a list of KLs as existing in January, 1944, but the COLUMBIA-HAUS has been known as a Gestapo HQ with facilities for pre-trial detention. It is most likely still that and not a KL. BERLIN ALEXANDERPLATZ. Reported to have had 20,000 men in its cells waiting transfer to KLs. This may be the COLUMBIA HAUS reported above. <u>SS Units and Establishments in the Vicinity.</u> Ergänzungsstelle der Waffen-SS (NW10, Wilsnackerstr.3) SS Hauptfürsorge- und Versorgungsamt (Reichsministerium d. Innern, NW7, Unter den Linden 72) SS Standortkommandatur (W15, Meineckestr.10) SS Kleiderkasse (Kölnischer Fischmarkt 4) - now evacuated to BAD SARROW SS Wachbataillon 1 (Berlin-Lankwitz, Leonorenstr.17) SS Hauptsanitätslager (Berlin-Lichtenberg, Rittergutstr.19-21) SS Kraftfahrzeugamt (Berlin-Lichterfelde) SS Kraftfahr Ausbildung- und Ersatzabteilung (Berlin-Lichterfelde, Finkenstein-allee) Hauptwirtschaftslager der Waffen-SS (Südende, Turmstr.4) SS und Polizeigericht (Berlin-Schmargendorf, Davoserstr.1) Auskunftsstelle für Kriegsverluste der Waffen-SS (Berlin-Siemensstadt, Siemensdamm 82-84) Beauftragter für den Diensthundewesen der Waffen-SS (Berlin-Stieglitz, Bökequell)

BERLIN (Brandenburg) (cont'd.)	SS Lazarett at HOHENLYCHEN, N of Berlin SS Panzer Gruppe Ausbildungs- und Ersatz Bataillon 1 at SPREENHAGEN, near Berlin SS Lager at STAHNSDORF (TELTOW, Berlin) SS Strafvollzugslager at LUDWIGSFELDE (Kr. TELTOW)
BERNAU (Brandenburg)	Near Berlin Last reported March, 1938. Believed to be no longer in operation.
BERNAU (Oberbayern)	Identified in 1943. Last reported January, 1944. **Location and Size** Near ROSENHAIN, Chiemsee. Camp "stretches over several miles towards the Alps". **Inmates** Arbeitslager for men; including:- Gerüchtserzähler (rumour mongers) Schwarzhörer (listeners to foreign broadcasts) Schwarzschlächter (black market butchers) Other Volksschädlinge (anti-social elements) According to a German newspaper dated December, 1943, there were 1,400 inmates, all from Bayern and the Protectorate, "as the camp serves these territories". **Remarks** Its sister institution for women is in LAUFEN/Salzach SS china porcelain enterprises are reported to draw labour from here as well as from DACHAU, but this is not confirmed.
BERNBURG (Magdeburg-Anhalt)	Near DESSAU. Believed to be in operation as detention centre of unknown classification.
BEYENBURG (Rheinland)	Also reported as BAYENBURG near WUPPERTAL. Last reported May, 1938. BAYENBURG is not listed in the directory; BEYENBURG exists as suburb of WUPPERTAL.
BIALYSTOK (Poland)	In region incorporated into Ostpreussen as a Regierungsbezirk. There is a KL at ZASCIANEK, very close to BIALYSTOK. Reported as a segregating camp for expropriated Poles, with 40,000 inmates.

BILIN
(Czechoslovakia)	Not definitely confirmed

BIRKENAU (BRZEZINKI)
(SW Poland)	Type
	    Special KL and annihilation camp for women reported here.
	Inmates
	    Reported to be mostly Hungarian Jews.
	Remarks
	    Most likely controlled by AUSCHWITZ, where Jews are sent to keep the 4 crematoria busy.

BIRNBAUM (MIEDZYCHOD)
(Poland)	Possibly Straflager: a forced labour camp was reported in this area.

BISCHOFSHOFEN
(KAZIMIERZ-BISKUPI)
(Central Poland)	Near KONSKIE. Reported in 1939/1940 as KL for priests from W Poland.

BISCHOFSGRÜN
(Bayern)	Telephone directory (1941) lists "Strafgefangenenlager" here.

BLANKENHAIN
(Thüringen)	15 Km. S WEIMAR: last reported May, 1938.

BLARICUM
(Holland)	Camp reported but not confirmed a KL.

BOCCHE DI CATARO	See BAR

BOCHNIA
(Poland)	40 Km. ESE KRAKAU.
	Type
	    May not be a KL; a ghetto is reported in this town and may be identical with reported camp.
	Inmates
	    Number estimated at 8,000.

BOCHUM VI
(Westfalen)	Reported before 1939 as KL. The VI may imply that there are other camps in the vicinity; note, however, that Bochum is in Wkr.VI.

BODCZENTIN
(Poland)	Type
	    There is a ghetto in this town, which may be identical with reported KL.
	Inmates
	    One report estimates 1,000 inmates there.

BOGEN "For intellectuals".
(N Norway)

BOGUMIN (Polish) or See ODERBERG
BOHUMIN (Czech)

BOJANOW (BOJANOWO) 70 Km. NNW BRESLAU. Reported as KL
(W Poland) for women; as special KL for nuns; as
"Dulag for monks and nuns".

BOJNICE Not confirmed.
(Slovakia)

BOLLAN Near ALESUND.
(Norway)

BOMIECHOWEK I Near MODLIN; KL.
(Poland)

BOMIECHOWEK II Near WARSCHAW; KL for Jews.
(Poland)

BÖRGERMOOR See EMSLAND

BÖRNICKE Possibly Straflager; may be connected
(Brandenburg) with SACHSENHAUSEN. Last reported
March, 1938.

BÖTZOW Near SPANDAU. Last reported in
(Brandenburg) March, 1938 with 800 inmates.

BOUGUENAIS Inmates
(France, Loire- The CAMP DES LANDES was reported
Inferieure) in June, 1943, to have 233 "communists" and 30 black marketeers,
"syphilitic prostitutes and anti-
social elements" as inmates.

BOZANOWO 15 Km. N of RAWICZ; probably
(Poland) identical with BOJANOW.
KL for clergy.

BRAETZ-SCHWIEBUS Auffangslager
(Brandenburg) Believed to be in operation.

A26

BRANDENBURG	Near BERLIN. Old Zuchthaus
KL 1933-35.
Reported in operation in spring, 1941
"for Jewish intellectuals"; probably
not in operation now.

BRAUNSBERG	Location
(Ostpreussen)	 Near HEILIGENBEIL; possibly
identical with TOLKEMIT.
Type
  Strafanstalt to which KL was
attached.
  Last known to be in operation
in 1935.

BRAUWEILER	Reported, May, 1938, to be near BAD
(Rheinland)	KREUZNACH, but may be identical with
BRAUNWEILER near KÖLN.

BRAUNWEILER	10 Km. W of Köln.
Used as collecting point for KL
transports in November, 1938.

BREEDENE	Detention camp located there;
(Belgium)	possibly KL, but reported as
"occupied by prisoners".

BREENDONCK	Inmates
(Belgium)	 "Jews and Gentiles"; the latter
serve definite terms after release
from a regular prison.
  Hostages (Rabbi ULLMANN) kept
here.
Capacity
  500 inmates reported in September,
1943.
  Camp was to be enlarged to hold
2,000.
Personalities
  Commandant: OSBF SCHMIDT, in
office since January, 1944; (there is
a Polizei-Major Dr. SCHMIDT reported
in MALINES)
  HSF HUMPERT, probably connected
with this camp.
  Two Jewish inmates, OBLER and
KESSLER, and two Belgian SS men,
WEISS and DOBOTTE "excel in sadism".
  The entire staff was reported in
July, 1943, as consisting of 1 Major,
1 Lt., and about 50 German and
Belgian SS men.

BREMEN   A camp for Jews, Poles and Spaniards
                                 reported near this town in January,
                                 1944.
                                 Dienststelle SS Fürsorgeoffizier

BRENS   Near GAILLAC. 365 women, political
    (France (Tarn)   prisoners, prostitutes, black market
                                 offenders reported there.

BRESCHAN (BREZANY)   There are 3 towns by this name, plus
    (Czechoslovakia)   a BRESCHAN/EGER, in Czechoslovakia.
                                 It is reported, however, that inmates
                                 of this camp were employed in the
                                 building of the PARDUBITZ airfield.
                                 The German command at this camp is
                                 assisted by former Gendarmes.

BRETSTEIN   Near MAUTHAUSEN.
    (Oberdonau)   Believed in operation.

BRETTVEDT   Previously reported as BREDTVEDT.
    (Norway)   Said to be camp for former members
                                 of NS (Norwegian Nazi Party) who
                                 have broken with the party.

BREZANY   See BRESCHAN

BROMBERG   Reported as camp for Polish child
    (Poland)   hostages, 6-12 years.

BRUAL-RHEDE   See EMSLAND

BRUCK/MUR   Camp reported for those evading
    (Styria)   compulsory labour.

BRÜNN (BRNO)   An internment camp, located at a
                                 student college reported there.
                                 SS Panzer Grenadier Ausbildung
                                 und Ersatz Bataillon 10.

BRZEZINKI   See BIRKENAU

BUCHAU   Location
    (Württemberg)   14 Km. W of BIBERACH.
                                 Type
                                     Alleged to be for Volksschädlinge
                                 (anti-social elements).

BUCHENWALD
(Thüringen)

Near WEIMAR. Railway station SCHÖNDORF

Type
   Probably identical with KLs referred to as ERFURT and DORNBURG. Definitely KL.

Inmates
   November, 1940, 24,000 inmates were reported there.
   A report of 1942 speaks of 12-14,000 inmates, among them 1,300 Czechs, 800 Poles, 2,000 Russians (in special enclosure), "and a few Yugoslavs, Frenchmen and Dutchmen".
   January, 1944, 20,000 inmates were reported to be in the camp.

Guard
   March, 1940, SS guards moved out, and were replaced by blue-uniformed men from the Justizverwaltung (Ministry of Justice). Late 1940, discharged Waffen-SS men again took over.
   1942, it was reported that the guard consisted of 700-800 SS guards, including 100 officers.

SS Units in the Vicinity

SS Nachschublager
SS Panzer Ausbildung und Ersatz Bataillon
SS Kraftfahr Ausbildung und Ersatz Bataillon
SS Panzer Grenadier Ersatz Bataillon 4 (WEIMAR)
Panzer Grenadier Bataillon Totenkopf III
Feldgendarmerie Kompagnie Kommando Stab Reichsführer SS "Hegewald" (WEIMAR)
Feldgendarmerie Einheiten der Leibstandarte ADOLF HITLER
SS Feldpostprüfstelle, Ausbildungsstelle und Motorgendarmerieschule

Personalities

E. Franz VOSS	SS OGF	commandant (1944)
FLORSTEDT	SS SBF	1 Lagerführer (1944)
SCHOBER(?T)	SS HSF	2 Lagerführer (1944) Also referred to as Deputy CO.
Hermann PISTER	SS SF	commandant (Dec. 1943)
Otto BARNEWALD	SS SBF	Leiter d. Lagerverw.
Otto FOERSCHNER	SS SBF	
WEISENBOLN(?)	SS HSF	1 Lagerführer (1937-1938)
PLAZA	SS OSF	(Dec. 1943)
Heinrich KRONE	HSF	
Dr. HOVEN	HSF	Garrison M.O.

BUDZYN
(Poland)

12 Km. SE of CHODZIEZ. Reported as "Dulag" for civilians; not confirmed.

BUKOWA

See KIELCE

BURG HOHENECK
(Hannover)

In Harz mountains.
Youth detention and correction camp reported in 1943.

BURG HOHNSTEIN
(Sachsen)

Location
 May be HOHNSTEIN, Sächs.Schweiz.
Type
 Identified until 1938 as KL; later reported as Stalag IVA (PW camp) guarded by Landesschützen. Believed to be no longer in operation as KL.

C

CERWICA
(Poland)

Reported as KL.

CHAIMOVA
(Slovakia)

Not confirmed.

CHARLEVILLE-MEZIERES
(France, Ardennes)

In September, 1942, a large concentration camp for Jews reported near this town.

CHAUVAILLES
(France, Saone-et-Loire)

Not confirmed as German or Vichy operated KL; may be detention camp of another type.

CHELM
(Poland)

District of LUBLIN.
Type
    Reported as "punitive camp for forced labor."
SS Troops in the vicinity
    SS Kavallerie Ersatz Abteilung, SS Reiter Ausbildung Schwadron.

CHELMNO

See KULM.

CHIOS
(Greece)

Not confirmed.

CHLUDOW
(Poland)

Reported in 1939/40; KL "for priests" probably not in operation since 1940.

CHOJNICE

See KONITZ.

CHRUBIESZOW
(Poland)

Forced Labour camp with enclosures for Jews.

CIECHANOW

See ZICHENAU.

COLDITZ

34 Km. SE of LEIPZIG.
Confirmed until 1941.

COMPIEGNE
(France)

Location
    Near Paris
Type
    Polizeihaftlager, but also reported to have section for British women internees from Channel Islands as well as section for Jews who were deported sometime during 1944.

CORFU
    (Greece)
Ionian Islands; KL stated to be "in the island of Lazarette, Corfu," reported with 600 inmates in July 43.
See also PAXOL.

CORINTH
See KORINTH.

CRETE
    (Greece)
Not confirmed.
Exact location unreported.

CRIMMITSCHAU
    (Sachsen)
Near ZWICKAU.
Existence confirmed in 1933.
Last reported May 38.

CZESTOCHOWA
See TSCHENSTOCHAU.

D

DABROWA (Poland)

Number of inmates estimated at 6,000.

DACHAU (Bayern)

Location
16 km NW München; the actual site of the camp has been reported as being 10 to 12 km NE of DACHAU on the right bank of the river Amper.

Inmates
From 1940-43 the number of inmates varied between 12,000 and 30,000; an undated report gives the following breakdown:

Germans
Political:	400
Berufsverbrecher: (Habitual Criminals)	1000
Workshy, Bibelforscher (Religious Enthusiats)	800

Non-Germans
Belgians:	400
French:	500
Dutch:	300
Norwegian:	300
Czechs:	1000
Poles and Russians:	6000
Catholic Priests of various nationalities	800

In November 1941, 8,000 inmates were trained at the KL for factory work; 2,000 worked in the aircraft parts factory inside the camp.

In 1942 the camp is said to have been closed for at least a short period and exclusively used as Waffen-SS training centre, SS-TV barracks and replacement depot; the inmates are said to have been taken to MAUTHAUSEN and, according to some reports, possibly also to AUSCHWITZ AND NEUENGAMME.

These were "Jews, Communists, political suspects of the Wehrmacht, Italians and Spaniards."

In spring, 1943, the camp was reported as reopened.

While the end of 1943 another report claims 10,000 inmates at the same time.

Guards
Only about 300 SS guards for camp and outside working parties, all over 40 yrs. Foreman (Arbeitskapos) selected from Berufsverbrecher (Habitual criminals) but training units of nearby Waffen-SS could be called in for emergencies.

DACHAU (Continued)

Remarks
Adjacent to the KL punishment camp for Waffen-SS and Polizei with 1.400 to 1.600 inmates has been reported.
This seems to be an institution similar to the one in DANZIG-MATZKAU.

SS Units and establishments in the vicinity.
SS Standartkereich
SS Gewürzhof (SS Spice Farm)
SS Krautergarten (Herb Garden)
SS China porcelain manufacturing plant.
SS Hauptzeugamt
SS Hauptwirtschaftslager
SS Ausrustungswerk
SS Bekleidungswerk
HQ Bauinspektion Süd (Inspectorate of Construction "South.")
SS Bekleidungswerke (SS-Clothing Works)
SS Lazarett (SS Hospital)
GV Prüfstelle (Gesundheitsverzehrungsprüfstelle der Waffen-SS)(Functions unknown)
SS Waffenamt Prüfungswerkstätte (Ordnance testing centre)
SS Führer Schule der Verwaltung (SS School of Administration)(SBF MULLER)
SS Sanitätsschule
Waffentechnische Lehranstalt der Waffen-SS (Technical Ordnance Training Center) (OSF Otto ARRAS)
SS Totenkopf Stand. "Oberbayern" (SS-SF NOSTITZ. Formerly TV Sturmbann I. Oberbayern, a regional command.
Ers. Abt. SS Verwaltungsdienststab.
SS Flakausbildung und Ersatz Rgt. (SS AA. Training and Replacement Rgt.)
SS Wirtschafts Btl.
SS Ausbuilding und Ersatz Abteilung der Verwaltungs Dienste
Transport Offizier SS-"Süd" (Aussenstelle des TO-SS b. FHA, Transportdienststelle)
SS Rekrutenstandarte
SS Lazarett
Karstwehr-Ersatz Kompagnie
SS Lehrküche

Personalities

Name	Rank	Role
Martin WEISS	OSBF	commandant since Apr. 43.
GRUNEWALD	SBF	deputy commandant
Hans EICHELE	OSBF	Leiter der SS-Standortverwaltung (CO of SS Garrison Command)
Dr. BRACHTEL	HSF	Dr. at the camp.
Dr. WOLTER	HSF	Senior camp M.O.
Prof. BREUER		Psychiatrist
REDWITZ	HSF	Also reported as deputy commandant.

DACHAU (Continued)	Personalities (Continued)		
	KLAITENHOF	HSF	
	Otto REINECKE	USF	
	Sigmund RASCHER	USF	
	Previous commandants:		
	A. PIORKOWSKI	SBF	(reported Feb. 1942)
	LORITZ	OF	

(1940-43)

WEISS	?	Adjutant to PIORKOWSKI
HOFMANN	USF	1. Lagerführer
JAROLIM	USF	2. Lagerführer
REMMELE	HaScharF	1. Rapportführer
FRONAPFER	OScharF	2. Rapportführer
PFEIFER	OScharF	SS-kitchen
MAY	OScharF	Prisoners' kitchen
WAGNER	HaScharF	Laundry
PREISS	OScharF	Cell Leader
SCHLEMMER	OScharF	Cell Leader
ZEISS	HaScharF	Cell Leader) Brothers
ZEISS	HaScharF	Cell Leader)
REMETZ	OScharF	Cell Leader
NIEDERMAYER	OScharF	Cell Leader
TIEDCHEN		Gestapo Kommissar
STUMPF	USF	Politische Abteilung
ZILLE	HSF	Lagerführer until 1942, when he went to LUBLIN.

DANZIG

Type
Reported in January, 1944, as "segregating camp for expropriated Poles."
Inmates
5,000 people reported there.
SS Units in the Vicinity
Hauptwirtschaftslager der Waffen SS
Truppenwirtschaftslager der Waffen SS
SS und Polizei Gericht
Ergänzungsstelle der Waffen SS
(GOTENHAFEN, Adolf Hitlerplatz 10-12

DANZIG, District
Reported as KL "for priests"; May refer to STUTTHOF which has also been reported as such.
May also include PUTZIG and STEINBERG GOTENHAFEN.
See STUTTHOF and PUTZIG.

DANZIG-MATZKAU

Type
Called <u>Strafvollzugslager der SS und Polizei.I</u>
Inmates
Has SS prisoners convicted from six months - one year. These work on docks together with French PWs but do not speak to them. Many joined 999th Div.

DEBICA
(Poland)

Type
  KL.
SS Units and establishments in the Vicinity.
  Textile Mills
SS Truppenubungsplatz Heidelager (Post PUSTKOW)
SS Sturmgeschützersatz Batt. 9 (Replacements for Assault Gun Battery 9, HJ Div.)
SS Fahrzeugersatzeinheit (SS Motor Replacement Unit)
5"Ringe" (48 companies of 4 platoons of 30 men each)
SS Kavallerie Regt. 1
SS   "   "   2
SS Polizei Regiment 1
SS   "   "   2
SS   "   "   3
SS Infanterie Regiment 8
SS   "   "   10
Elements of the SS-Totenkopf Division and of Estnische SS-Freiwilligen Division
Zentral Bauleitung der Waffen-SS und Polizei
SS Ausbildung und Ersatz Btl. 33
SS Panzer Grenadier Ausbildung und Ersatz Btl. 36
SS Depot (SS-BF und Genmaj. d. W.-SS Bernard VOSS)
Personalities
  Wilhelm SCHITTLI   HSF Commandant
    (or SCHITLI)
  MANSFELD   OSF Camp M.O.
SS Grenadier Ausbildungs und Ersatz Regiment 14 (GALIZIEN Ausb.Regt.1) at HEIDELAGER
Hauptzeugamt der Waffen SS
SS Wach Bn 5
SS Standort Verwaltung

DEDINJE
(Yugoslavia)

See BELGRADE

DHOMOKOS
(Greece)

Location
  Phthiotis Phokis
Type
  KL reported with 565 inmates in June 1944.

DIDOSTXDION
(Greece)

See MYTILENE

DIDYMOTIKHON
(Greece)

In Western Thrace: reported as KL.

DJAKOVO
(Greece)

In Croatia: KL reported in the vicinity.

DOBRZYCA
(Poland)

Location
    On KROTOSZYN-PIESZEW DRZYST Railway line.
    26 Km. from KROTOSZYN.
Type
    Reported as KL.

DOBRZYN
(Poland)

Location
    On Vistula, 28, Km. NW of PLOCK.
Type
    KL. Probably identical with PLOCK Camp.

DOMBAAS
(Norway)

Also reported as DOMBAS: opened late 1941.

DOMBURG
(Holland)

Reported in February 1944.
Type
    "Erziehungsheim". Disciplinary camp for people who refused to work on Zeeland Fortifications.
Inmates
    Inmates include OT people.

DOMOKOS
(Greece)

KL reported there with 565 inmates in June.
Camp run by Germans.

DORNBURG
(Magdeburg-Anhalt)

Location
    Probably in ANHALT near BRÖDEL, but possibly near JENA. In the latter case it may be close to, or identical with BUCHENWALD.
    Has also been reported as DORNBERG near DESSAU.
Inmates
    Last reported in March 1938 as having 800 inmates.

DÖRPEN, WALCHUM

See EMSLAND

DOULLENS
(France, Somme)

Type
    Reported in September, 1941, to be a detention camp for black marketeers.
Inmates.
    Said to have contained Frenchmen who were generally transferred to labour units of the OT.

DRANCY
(France, Seine)

Type
    KL for Jews of various countries, both sexes and all ages; all wear yellow star.

DRANCY (Continued)　　Capacity
　　　　2,500-3,000 inmates though it is
　　said that as many as 30,000 were here
　　at one time. 1,000 being sent to
　　Germany almost every month; in November,
　　1943, it was confirmed that they went
　　into OT, by January, 1944, about 30,000
　　are said to have passed through this
　　camp.
　　Remarks
　　　　In July, 1943, Beaune-La-Rolande camp
　　with only about 200 inmates was moved
　　there.
　　Guards
　　　　In summer, 1943, there were only five
　　Germans and 300 French guards at this
　　camp.
　　Personalities

BRUNNER	HSF	commandant
ROETHKE	OSF	exact position not known; reported as successor to a certain sadist named DANNECKER
BRUCKNER	Schaft	Often seen with BRUNNER

DREWNICA
　(Poland)

　　Near CHELM.
　　Reported January, 1943.
　　Also reported as Forced Labor Camp.

DÜREN
　(Rheinland)

　　27 Km. E. of AACHEN.
　　Not confirmed. Reported May 38.

DÜRKHEIM

　　See BAD DÜRKHEIM

DUN-SUR-AVON
　(France)

　　A camp of 100 wooden huts was reported
　　on Route Nationale 153 near this town
　　in July, 1944; 400 men of the *Milice*
　　are said to be stationed there
　　engaged in "torturing prisoners."

DYLE
　(Poland)

　　S of LUBLIN; reported as KL.

DZIALDOWO

　　See SOLDAU.

DZIESIATA
　(Poland)

　　S of LUBLIN; reported as "permanent KL"

DZEZINKA

　　Near AUSCHWITZ
　　30,000 inmates reported to have been
　　liquidated on a single day in or prior
　　to October, 1943.
　　Possibly identical with BRZEZINKI
　　(BIRKENAU).

E

ECROUVES
(France, Meurthe-et-Moselle)

Between TOUR and ECROUVES.
Called Centre de surveille: exact status of the camp is not known.
In August, 1943, 145 people were interned there for "political reasons":-
    14 as black marketeers,
    21 women offenders against common law,
    42 men interned "by order of the Germans".

EDESSA (EDESSIS)
(Greece)

Macedonia: KL reported here with 7,000 inmates in January 1943.

EGGEMØN
(Norway)

Near RØNEROSS: reported in 1943.

EILPE
(Westfalen)

Near ALTENA: not listed in the directory. Last reported in 1936.

EKNE
(Norway)

Location
    Near TRONDHJEM.
Inmates
    About 200.
Remarks
    Reported in 1943.
    According to another report, it was opened in February 1944 as the Volla prison was no longer adequate for the Sipo.

EILA
(Bayern)

Near MÜNCHEN: believed no longer in operation.
For units nearby, see STADELHEIM.

ELBING
(Ostpreussen)

Formerly OSTPREUSSEN, now DANZIG-WESTPREUSSEN.
Probably dissolved.

ELEUSIS
(Greece)

ATHENS area; unconfirmed report of a KL.

ELLECOM
(Holland)

"For Jews and Aryans" also "political prisoners".

ELSINORE
(Denmark)

KL for Communists and "Dangerous Individuals" reported here.

EMBIRIKOS ASYLIUM
(Greece)

Reported as a reformatory for young women holding 100 inmates, but may well be a KL.

EMSLAND
(Hannover)

A group of camps with administrative headquarters at PAPENBURG. Commonly referred to as PAPENBURG-ESTERWEGEN or "Moorlager" (as a general term).

While a 1934/5 report knows of only five, fourteen camps were reported in 1943, but these camps are in operation "according to needs". They are not all of the same type, and the following have been identified. (Roman numerals are official German designations):-

I. BÖGERMOOR
Strafgefangenenlager: reported in May 1943 as having 1,500 inmates.
SA guards.
SA Truppführer JOHANNIS reported there, 1940.

II. ASCHENDORFER MOOR
SK-lager with 1,700 inmates reported i in 1940. At the same time SA Stuf. SAUTHOF was reported there.
The camp was last reported in May, 1943.
Guards are SA.

III. RUAL-RHEDE
SK-lager.
Last reported in November 1937 as having SS guards.

IV. DÖRPEN, WALCHUM
Type
Strafgefangenenlager: referred to by inmates as WALCHUM.
The camp seems to be primarily for war criminals (Kriegsverbrecher or KV)
Guards
SA men from all parts of Germany who are picked for their cruelty. They are called "Blaue" because of their blue uniforms.
Remarks
The work, cutting peat, is supervised by farmers and farmhands from nearby who are called "Kneiske" (From Kneis, Dutch for Knecht - farm hand) and distinguished by white caps.
Personalities
    BUSS   Oberwachtmeister
    ERMISCH   "
    KLEINE-DÖPKE   Platzmeister
    AUSSEM, Christian Commandant in 1940.

V. NEUSUSTRUM
Last reported in May, 1938 as having SS guards.

VII. ESTERWEGEN
Known as "Moorlager".
Inmates
    1936. Berufsverbrecher (habitual

EMSLAND (Contd.)

criminals) who wore B.V. on their Jackets. Some inmates wore red stripes on back and sleeves.

Type

SK-lager with 2000 inmates in 1940.

Also reported as Straflager for Poles, Jews and Gypsies.

A Sonderlager for soldiers was said to be only attached.

Guards

SS men of Wachtruppe "Ostfriesland" (1936).

In May 1943, camp was last reported as having SA guards.

Personalities

LIEDTKE, Harry	Wachtmeister (before 1942)
SCHMIDT	? Lagerleiter
SCHWARDT	OSF (reported December, 1943)

Other camps of various types belonging to this group are:

OBERLANGEN/Ems.
Reported in November 1937 as having SS guards.

PAPENBURG
Last reported in May 1943, as having SS guards.
2,000 Jews and Poles are said to be detained here.

LATHEN
Last reported in 1936 as having SS guards.

KRONDORF
WATENSTEDT
WESERMOOR
HEMSEN

The relationship of the following camps to EMSLAND is not known:-

Gefangenenarbeitskommando ABELITZMOOR
AURICH,
Arbeitslager FEDDERWARDEN,
Moorkommando OLDENBRUCK in STRÜCKHAUSEN
Gefangenenlager WIESMOOR.

Either some of these or other unidentified camps are Russian PW camps, which were reported by former inmates as being guarded by Landesschützen.

EMSLAND (contd.)
Units in this area
Sturmbann IV "Ostfriesland" represents the SS Totenkopf command in this region.

Personalities
For HQ personalities see PAPENBURG.

ERFURT
(Halle-Merseburg)
Last reported in May 1938.
Possibly identical with another camp. (See BUCHENWALD).

ESPELAND
(Norway)
Location
20 km. from BERGEN; also reported as ESPELUND.
Inmates
In December 1943 number was given as 200.
Remarks
This camp was to be enlarged while the KL at ULVEN was to be abandoned; the two have the same commander reported as HELENIA or HOLENIA.
The camp administration is said to be German.

ESTERWEGEN
See EMSLAND.

EUTIN
(Schleswig-Holstein)
Reported before 1939, 11 km. North of LÜBECK.
Reported 1936 near Neumünster.

FAREVEJLE
(Denmark)

Built on Lammefjord.
High school building; believed to be in operation.

FALLERSLEBEN

See ARBEITSDORF FALLERSLEBEN.

FALSTAD
(Norway)

Location
    8 miles NE TRONHJEM.
Type
    Referred to as "Gestapolager" and definitely German-operated.
Inmates
    In March, 1943, 354 inmates, 11 of them women, reported there. Late in 1943 115 inmates reported as having been sent to Germany.

FARGE
(Hannover)

Location
    23 Km. Northwest of BREMEN.
Type
    Reported in 1943 as Arbeitslager; one report claims the camp to be divided into
    (a) Germans (Volksschädlinge?)
    (b) "Europeans" including Baltic inmates.
    (c) Poles.
    (d) Russians.
Remarks
    Possibly same as HASTEDT.

FECHENBACH
(Bayern)

Probable location 30Km. south of ASCHAFFENBURG.
Reported before 1939; not confirmed.

FERINCANCE
(Yugoslavia)

KL reported there.
Commanders:
    Sr Lt. Filip HERMANS and Lt. Adam TISLER.

FISCHERN
(Sudetenland)

10 Km. west of KARLSBAD.
Confirmed in 1942. There are in KARLSBAD an SS Lazarett and an SS Genesungsheim.

FLORINA
(Greece)

Macedonia; KL reported with unknown capacity.
Used by Germans and Bulgarians.

FLOSSENBURG
(Bayern)

Near WEIDEN.
Last reported in June 1943 as having 2,000 inmates.
Also reported as FLOSSENBURG and in the latter case possibly belonging to the

F

FLOSSENBURG (Contd.) Emsland Group. There is no FLOSSENBURG listed in the directory.
Personalities:

Egon ZILL	SBF	commandant (formerly at NATZWEILER)
Dr. SCHNABEL	SBF	Garrison M.O.
FRITZSCH	HSF	deputy commandant.
KOERMANN	USF	
Willy FASSBENDER	USF	

Commandant in 1941: SBF KUNSTLER

FOEHENHEIN (Hessen) Near OFFENBACH. Last reported May 1938.

FORT VII a See POSEN.

FRANKENSTEIN (Schlesien) Near NEISSE. Last reported in 1936.

FRANKENTHAL (Bayern)
Location.
  Probably in Pfalz; possibly near REICHENBERG in Schlesien.
Type.
  Reported as "Dulag" until 1938; believed to be in operation.

FREISTADT (FRYSZTAT) (SW Poland) Reported October, 1943. Reported as segregating camp "for expropriated Poles."

FREJUS (France) Marseille region; reported as "KL for civilians" in March, 1943.

FRESNES (France, Seine) Jail used as clearing house for Allied "evaders" and for French.
3000 inmates including 600 women reported there.
Remarks
  Controlled by the Gestapo.

FRIEDENSHÜTTE (HUTA ZGODA) (Poland, Upper Silesia) A Forced Labor Camp reported there.

FRØSLEV (Denmark) Near PADBORG. A new internment camp reported there in August, 1944; possibly KL now. See also HORSERØD.

F

FRYDRYCHOWKA See LEMBERG

FRYSZTAT See FREISTADT.

FÜRSTENBERG Identical with RAVENSBRÜCK and probably
(Mecklenburg) identical with UCKERMARK.
In December. 1942, "female SS guards"
from this camp are reported as having
paraded through SACHSENHAUSEN.
In addition a Police School "FÜRSTENBERG"
is also reported.
Estonian Volunteers probably trained there
during the winter of 42/43.

FÜRSTENBURG Probably reported in error for FÜRSTEN-
BERG; information on this camp is id-
entical with that on RAVENSBRÜCK.
There is an SS Lehrschwadron der Kavall-
erieverwaltung at DAHLMSHOHJ nr. F/ODER
and an SS Ausbildungstager at F/ODER.

FUHLSBÜTTEL See HAMBURG.

G

GAILLIN — Reported as Camp de Gaillin, Angers region. Not confirmed as KL.

GARCZYN (NW Poland) — Reported as correctional camp for youths.

GARWOLIN (Central Poland) — Reported in November, 1943, as "punitive camp for forced labour."

GDANSK — See DANZIG.

GHOUDI (GOUDI) — Athens Area; KL reported with 521 hostages from KALAMSS in Oct 1943. This camp is now stated to be closed down.

GINSHEIM (Hessen) — Probably MAINZ-GINSHEIM; reported before 1939; not confirmed.

GINZHEIM (Hessen) — Near WIESBADEN; last reported May 1938. Possibly identical with GINSHEIM. (GINZHEIM not listed in the directory).

GLASMOOR — A camp GLASMOOR was reported in 1936 as "certain to exist". Unlocated.

GLEIWITZ (Schlesien) — Reported as having moved here from WURZBURG in April, 1943. British inmates. Camp may be a Zwangsarbeitslager. An SS ordnance depot is located in SCHRAU bei GLEIWITZ. SS Lazarett in GLEIWITZ.

GLOWNA (Poland) — Reported as KL.

GLÜCKSTADT (Schleswig-Holstein) — 45 Km. northwest of HAMBURG. Last reported May 1938.

GOLCZA (Poland) — Reported as KL.

GOLDFIALS (Baltic states) — Believed in operation.

GONDA (Holland) — Reported as KL for women.

GORCZIN
(Poland)
Suburb of POSEN.
Reported in January, 1944, as segregating camp for Polish labour.

GÖRNAU
(ZGIERZ)
(Poland)
10 Km. north of LITZMANNSTADT; reported as KL.

GORNA GRUPA
See OBERGRUPPE.

GORZYCE
(SW Poland)
Reported in October, 1943, as segregating camp for "expropriated Poles".

GOTTESZELL
(Bayern)
30 Km. ENE of STRAUBING.
Said to be for women; last reported April 1937.

GRÄFENHAINICHEN
(Halle-Merseburg)
44 Km. NE of HALLE; reported before 1939.

GRÄFENHEINICHEN
(Sachsen)
Near Grimma.
Last reported in May 1938. Probably identical with GRÄFENHAINICHEN.

GRAJEWO
60 Km. SSW of SUWALKI, just south of old East Prussian border.
Reported as segregation camp and KL.

GRASSE
(France, Alpes Maritimes)
According to a report from January, 1944, a KL was being set up at the PLATEAU NAPOLEON.

GRAUDENZ
(GRUDZIADZ)
(Poland)
Reported as KL.
See also OBERGRUPPE.

GRCZYN
(Poland)
Reported as a reformatory camp for young Poles.

GRIEBO
(Magdeburg)
Kreis ZERBST; KL or Straflager; not confirmed.

GRIESHEIMERSLAND
(Hessen)
Near GRIESHEIM.
Last reported in 1936.

GRINI
(Norway)

Former women's prison, opened May/June, 1941.

Inmates

Inmates from ÅNEBY HAKADAL transferred there.

December, 1943, about 2,000 inmates, 100 of whom were women.

700 said deported to Germany in late 1943, but number of inmates still believed 2,000 early in 1944 owing to new influx.

800 political Norwegian prisoners reported to have been moved recently to soldiers' barracks at BARDV airfield.

Personalities

(From a supplement to a report of 7 August 1943).

DEUTZER	?	Lagerkommandant; born 1898; 1.78m tall; blond, fat.
REINHARDT	SBF	"Gestapo"
ZEIDLER	HSF	"Gestapo"; permanently stationed there.
KOCH	OSF	Gestapo; permanently stationed there. A Karl Otto KOCH SF reported as C.O. there in 1943, formerly at BUCHENWALD.
JØNICHEN	OSF	Gestapo; permanently stationed there; in administration.
REICH	OSF	Gestapo; permanently stationed there; in administration.
JENZER	USF	
KUNTZ	USF	
KUNTZE	USF	
LENZER	USF	
NIEBEL	USF	Connected with Bauleitung (Work's Directorate)
SCHWARTZ	USF	
SEIDEL	USF	
STANGE	USF	
BLATNER	Oschaf	
NUNZ	Oschaf	
NEMITZ	Oschaf	
SCHWARZ	Oschaf	
STANGE	Haschaf	
WARNECKE	Haschaf	
HEILEMANN	Schaf	
KUNTZE	Schaf	
LÜDTKE	Stuschaf	
BALABANOFF	("a Russian")	
CLAFFY	("a Dane")	

GROSSENROHRHEIM (Hessen)

Near DARMSTADT.
For women.
Believed to be in operation.

GROSSROSEN (Schlesien)

Location
    23 Km. S. LIEGNITZ.
Type
    KL, reported in 1938, and in 1943 as being still in operation.
Inmates
    In 1938 women inmates from MORINGEN were transferred to this camp.
    February 1943, 140 Austrians and 3,500 Russian PWs arrived at this camp. Special treatment and gas chambers awaited Russian commissars. The other PWs were hardly better off, and 60 - 80 deaths sometimes occurred in one day.
    July, 1943, some Polish inmates were reported to be in the camp.
    August, 1943. Inmates were put to work in quarries.
SS units in the vicinity
    Elements of SS Freiwilligen BOSNISCH-HERZEGOWINISCHE Gebirgs-Division "Kroatien".
    Elements of SS Grenadier Ersatz Btl. "Ost".
SS Infanterie Rgt. 4 (Mot).
Personalities

ROEDEL	HSF	Commandant until Apr 43
GRAY	HSF	Commandant from Apr 43
HENNEBERG	OSF	Verwaltungsführer
STOERZINGER	OSF	1 Company
THUMANN	USF	Lagerführer until Apr 43
ERZBERGER	OSF	Lagerführer from Apr 43
LINDSTEDT	Oschaf	SS Clothing store
OTTOHALL	Uschaf	SS Handicrafts
MARIENFELD	Uschaf	Inmates' kitchen
ESCHNER, Helmuth	Uschaf	I Rapportführer
SCHRAMMEL, Erich	Rottenfü.	II Rapportführer
WITTE	Rottenfü.	Blockführer
REMMELING	Rottenfü.	Blockführer
SCHRAMM	Rottenfü.	Blockführer
SCHWARZE	Uschaf	Arbeitsführer

GRUNDAUS (Ostpreussen)

Near KÖNIGSBERG.
Last reported in May 1938.
Not listed in the directory.

GRUDUADZ

See GRAUDENZ & OBERGRUPPE

GRÜNHAINICHEN (Sachsen)

Also reported as HAINICHEN.
Last reported March, 1938.

GURS
(France, Basses Pyrenees)

Capacity
According to a report of April, 1943, there are about 6,000 inmates, 2,000 of whom are Jews.

An undated report, conflicting with above figures, claims that 7,000 Jews are detained there, mostly German, and the camp has held up to 10,000.

Loyalist Spaniards detained there are said to need a request from the present Spanish government to be released.

Remarks
Camp was to be "cleaned out" by November, 1943.

GUSEN See MAUTHAUSEN.

H

HAAREN (Holland)
Location
N BRABANT; see entry under HEEREN. Lower HAAREN, the large seminary, is possibly intended.
Inmates
Approximately 400 inmates reported.
Guards
SD, SS, (Ukranians) (and a few Dutch SS-men).
Personalities
The Commander HSF WACKE is said to be leaving or to have left already. The new CO is unknown.

HADJIKOSTA ORPHANAGE
See ATHENS

HAIDARI (Greece)
Athens area, 3 km outside of ATHENS.
Type
KL reported
Inmates
Reported to have:
March 1944 - 1,200
April 1944 - 3,100
July 1944 - 2,000
17th July - 1,500
Personalities
The commandant in March was SS (Obersturmbannführer) Major RADOMSKI

HAINEWALDE (Sachsen)
Reported May '38. Not confirmed.

HAINICHEN (Sachsen)
See GRÜNHAINICHEN

HALKIDA
See KHALKIS

HAMBURG
Identified 1943, but probably operating as early as 1934.
Location
Main camp at FUHLSBÜTTEL.
Located in, or connected with the old
Zuchthaus
Inmates
November, 1943, 4,000 inmates reported to be in the camp, including Jews.
Related Camp
Connected with FUHLSBÜTTEL is Mooraussenstation SCHILP, last reported in December 1943 with 3,000 inmates.
Overflow camps at:
BERGEDORF, 15 Km. SE of HAMBURG.
WITTMOOR (Possibly a *Straflager*. It was identified until 1938.)
NEUENGAMME (This camp has been reported as connected with Mooraussenstation SCHILP.

HAMBURG
(Cont'd.)

Inmates
650 Norwegians. The camp was also reported as being a KL with 3,000 inmates and in October, 1943, was said to be connected with a "Gefangenenanstalt für 3,000 - 4,000 politisch Verurteilte". Also in 1943, 7,000 inmates (including some Russian PWs) were reported to be held there. (It is also said that there is a gas chamber there).

SS Units in the vicinity
A Bauleitung of the Bauinspektion der Waffen-SS Reich Nord.

SS Wehrgeologen Ersatz Bn (HAMBURG-LANGENHORN).

Ergänzungsstelle der Waffen SS (HAMBURG-13, Mittelweg 38).

SS Standortkommandantur (HAMBURG-LANGENHORN, SS Kaserne, Lahnstr.).

SS und Polizei Gericht

SS Pferdesammel und Ersatzstelle (ISERBROOK).

Personalities

SCHITLI	Haschaf	Arrived in 1940 from SACHSENHAUSEN, with rank of USF and job as Lagerführer.
WEISS	HSF	Camp Commandant in 1940. Early 1943 transferred to DACHAU
PAULI	SBF	Replaced WEISS
LUETGEMEYER	OSF	

HAMBURG-BARMBECK

Reported in operation as KL late in 1943.

HAMMERSTEIN
(Pommern)

Near SCHLOCHAU: last reported in 1936.

HAREN
(Holland)

Near BASSUN: last reported in 1936: SS Guards.

HASSELT
(Belgium)

Province of LIMBURG; 400 inmates; possibly not a KL.

HASTEDT
(Hannover)

This may be an alternative name for FARG. It was last reported in March, 1938, as HALSTEET near BREMEN, a place which does not exist.

HAZEBROUCK
(France, Nord)
The status of this camp is uncertain, but 479 Jews were reported to be there on 20th May, 1944.
An OT organization under Frontführer BAUER was probably employing their labour.

HEDMARCK District
(Norway)
One camp has been reported as located here.

HEEREN
(Holland)
Reported to contain political suspects. Possibly identical with HAAREN and HAREN.

HEIDE
(Schleswig-Holstein)
Near Toenning: last reported in 1936.

HEILSBERG
(Ostpreussen)
64 km. S of KÖNIGSBERG. Reported before 1939.

HEILVAREENBEEK
(Holland)
In October, 1943, a "KL for Dutch youths" reported there.

HELA
(Danzig)
Near DANZIG.
Reported as military KL.
Inmates
  Wear triangular red armbands with black SAW (Sonder Aktion Wehrmacht).

HELENCW
(Poland)
Near LITZMANNSTADT.
Reported in July, 1942, as experimental camp for the improvement of the Nordic race; allegedly 500-700 Polish boys and girls there.

HELM
(Poland)
KL reported in area; may be identical with CHELM.

HELMNOK-DEBIA ESTATE
(Poland)
13 km. SE of KOLO, on the NER river.
KL for Jews.

HERTOGENBOSCH
(Holland)
Location
  NOORD-BRABANT, also known as DEN BOSCH. See also HUY; there is a possible relationship to HAAREN.
Type
  The HAAREN Seminary was requisitioned by the Germans as a KL.
Inmates
  Inmates from BUCHENWALD were transferred there. It was reported to have mainly Dutch inmates, including some hostages.

A53

HEUBERG
(Baden)

Type
Though this camp was reported as a KL from 1941-43, it is probably not one. HEUBERG was the training ground for the 999th Div.

Inmates
September, 1943, there were 14,000 soldiers in HEUBERG, all former inmates of KLs. Since they were to carry weapons, the Gestapo was removed and the treatment was improved.

Guards
SS and SA units formed the guard, when the camp was last reported in 1942.

HINZERT
(Rheinland)

Location
Near TRIER.

Type
Referred to as Sonderlager; reported in 1944.

Inmates
Mostly Luxemburgers, Hollanders and Flemings.

Remarks
8 barracks of double rooms, each room for 70-90 men. (Inmates have their heads shaven. Working parties go as far as SAARBURG. 22.10.43.)

Personalities
    SPORENBERG, Brother of SS General SPORRENBERG   OSF   Commandant
    Jakob SCHNEIDER USF Deputy commandant
    WIPPS "Doyen du camp" (Lagerältester) well treated by SS.

HIOS
See KHIOS

HOBEN
(Holland)
Not confirmed

HOBOKEN
(Belgium)
Near ANTWERP, but existence not confirmed. There is an Ersatz Kolo. der Waffen-SS in ANTWERP.

HOF
(Bayern)
Near WEIDEN; 600 inmates (criminal) Latest report, Aug.'38.

HOHENBRÜCK
(Pommern)

Location
30 Km. SE STETTIN.

Type
In operation in 1941; a report claiming the move of this camp to VULKAN WERFT in 1938 conflicts with PW report claiming that VULKAN WERFT was an independent camp, not a KL, and not in operation in May, 1941.

HOHENECK
See BURG HOHENECK.

HOHENSALZA (INOWROCLAW)	**Type** Reported in January, 1942, as KL, September, 1942, as "punitive camp for forced labour". January, 1944, as punitive transit camp. **SS Units in the vicinity.** There is an <u>SS-Arbeitsstab</u> in this town at Wiesenstrasse 47.
HOHNSTEIN	See BURG HOHNSTEIN.
HOLBECKSHOF (Rheinland)	Near ESSEN. KL for Jews (Sept. 42).
HORSERØD (Denmark)	**Location** Near HELSINGØR. **Type** Possibly still in operation as KL. for political prisoners, although reports of August 1944 said it was to be converted into a military camp for special training. **Remarks** According to one source the 720 inmates were to be transferred to a new KL. at FRØSLEV but another source claims that they were to be taken to the Vestre prison in KOPENHAGEN, one wing of which is administered by the Gestapo.
HOYERSWERDA (Niederschlesien)	**Location** At HOYERSWERDA and BERNSDORF. Regierungsbezirk Liegnitz. **Type** Probably not a KL but a Work Camp and a Sammellager (Collecting Centre).
HRUBIESZOW (SE Poland)	Reported in October 1943 as forced labour camp for Jews.
HUTA BELDON	See Beldon Hütte under BENTSCHEN
HUTA ZGODA	See FRIEDENSHÜTTE
HUY Fortress of (Belgium)	**Location** SW LIEGE. **Inmates** In November, 1942, 800 inmates were reported there: "political prisoners, priests, hostages, labour evaders", etc. September, 1943, the number was down to 400-550. Beginning January, 1944, the camp was emptied; some inmates were taken to S'HERTOGENBOSCH in April, 1944. According to information obtained in Aug., 1944, the camp at HUY was moved to ACHEL; inmates were classified as "civilian prisoners".

I

IPISTI
(Greece)

Phthiotis Phokis, near LAMIS; KL reported with 90 inmates in Feb 1944. Inmates were used for roadwork, etc.

INOWROCLAW

See HOHENSALZA.

J

JABBEKE (Belgium)
Said to be occupied by "Russian Prisoners".
Probably identical with SCHAERBEKE (part of Greater BRUSSELS).

JABLONOW (NW Poland)
Reported in October, 1943, as transit-camp for "expropriated Poles".

JARGEAU (France, Loiret)
Not confirmed as a KL.
October 1943, 188 Gypsies, 62 prostitutes and 5 labour evaders were reported to be in this camp.

JASENOVAC (Yugoslavia)
Croatia.
KL for Croats, Serbs, Moslems, Gypsies and Jews.
Capacity about 800.
Camp controlled by the Ustaski.
In February 1943 the camp was liquidated. The internees were ordered to dig their own graves and then shot.
Commandant "Ustaski" Lt. Ljubomir MILOS.

JASLO (SW Poland)
Reported to be a KL.

JAWORZNLA
See KIELCE.

JAWORZYN (Poland)
On the CHRZANOW-SOSNOWIEC Railway line.
A KL was reported there, but it is probably identical with JAWORZYNA.

JAWORZYNA (W Poland)
This camp was reported in July, 1943, to be a "punitive camp for forced labour".
January, 1944, the number of inmates was estimated to be 8,000.

JERNVATN (N Norway)

JERSEY (Channel Isles)
1,000 Russian civilians are reported to be at St. Brelade.

JEZIERNA (SE Poland)
This camp was reported in November, 1943 to be a KL for Jews.

JÖRSTADMOEN (Norway)
This camp had teachers and Norwegian officers as inmates, but it was reported as being "without political prisoners" in January, 1944.

JÜLICH 25 Km. NE of AACHEN.
(Rheinland) It was reported before 1939, but its existence is not confirmed.

JÜTERBOG 63 Km. S of BERLIN.
(Brandenburg) It was reported as a double camp, and is possibly being used for military offenders of the Army and Waffen-SS training centre located there.
1,200 inmates were there according to the last report in March 1938.
<u>SS Units in the vicinity</u>
    SS Artillerieschule.1. (SS Artillery School 1)

K

KÄFERTAL
 (Baden)

Probably located between MANNHEIM and HEIDELBERG.
Reported in February 1944 as camp for "Badoglio Italians".

KALLITHEA
 (Greece)

Reported as prison but may well be a KL.

KALKTURM
 (Rhineland)

WITTLICH near TRIER.
Believed to be in operation.

KAMBINOWSKI REGION
 (Poland)

Near WARSAW.
Forced Labour Camp reported there.

KARASJOK
 (Unlocated)

Only reported in connection with OSF MARTIN and USF LEHMANN, both reported as stationed there.
Not confirmed.

KARLSRUHE
 (Baden)

Believed to be in operation.

KASSEL
 (Hessen - Nassau)

Reported May 1938 as KL.
Possibly identical with KASSEL. MELSUNGEN.
SS units in the vicinity
  SS Hauptwirtschaftslager der Waffen SS (VIASSEL-BREITENBACH)
  SS und Polizei Gericht. Ergänzungsstelle der Waffen SS (KASSEL-WILHELMSHÖHE, Löwenbrückstr 10)

KASSEL-MELSUNGEN
 (Hessen - Nassau)

Probably at MELSUNGEN, 21 Km S KASSEL.
Was in operation until 1939; not in recent reports.

KATTOWITZ (KATOWICE)
 (Poland)

Reported in November, 1942, as transit camp.
A Polizeischule is located there.

KAZIMIERZ-BISKUPI

See BISCHOFSHOFEN.

KEMNA
 (Rhineland)

Near WUPPERTAL.
Last reported May 1938.

A59

KHAIDARI   See HAIDARI

KHALKIS (Greece)   Euboea; KL reported with 350 inmates July, 1944.

KHIOS (Greece)   Aegean Islands; KL reported near KHIOS.

KIEL (Schleswig-Holstein)   200 Norwegians reported in Sondergericht.

KIELBASIN (NE Poland)   Near GRODNO. Reported in 1943 as "punitive camp for forced labour" There is an SS Standortverwaltung in GRODNO.

KIELCE (Poland)   Reported in June, 1943.
Type
There are 9 Baudienstlager (Polish forced labour camps under RAD supervision) in this district:-
  4 at KIELCE
  1 at BUKOWA
  1 at JAWORZNIA
  1 at RYKOSZ
  1 at PIEKOSZOW
  1 at WIERZNIA?
SS Units in the Vicinity
Elements of the SS Polizei-division.
SS MG Ausbildungs Schwadron (Training Squadron).
SS Heimatpferdepark.

KIRZALI (Greece)   Reported to be under the control of Bulgarian authorities.

KISLAU (Baden)   **Location**
25 Km. from HEIDELBERG, near BRUCHSAL.
Type
Probably not a KL.
It was reported before 1939.
Later it was reported as a camp for ex-members of the French Foreign Legion.
Inmates
900.

KLAGENFURT
(Austria)
Carinthia.
Capacity has been placed at 14,000 by German Sources. There is an SS and Waffen-Junkerschule in KLAGENFURT.

KLETY
(Czechoslovakia)
Not confirmed.

KOBLENZ-KARMELITA
(Rheinland)
Possibly identical with Zuchthaus there.

KOBLENZ-KARTHAUSE
(Rheinland)
Possibly identical with Zuchthaus there.
KL reported May, 1938.

KOCHEL
(Bayern)
This camp is used for Austrian political prisoners.

KOLBERG
(Pommern)
(SS Strafvollzugslager) An SS punishment camp has been reported here.

KOLDYRZEWO
(E Poland)
Near BARANOWICZE.
Reported as KL.

KOLDING
Near FLENSBURG
Type
　Wehrmachtshaftanstalt and Strafvollstreckungszug.
Inmates
　Political prisoners of armed forces with sentences up to 6 months and ordinary prisoners up to 6 weeks.
　"Danish partisans of both sexes are awaiting trial here".
Guards
　SS guards (January, 1944).
SS Units in the Vicinity
　SS Feldpostprüfung, Zweigstelle NORD (FLENSBURG, Grossestr.26)
　SS Passierscheinzweigstelle (FLENSBURG, Halle des Hauptbahnhofes)

KOMOTINI
(Greece)
Western Thrace; KL established by Bulgarians.
Capacity unknown.

KONIGSHÜTTE (KROLEWSKA HUTA)
(Poland)

Was reported in November, 1943 as a "punitive camp for forced labour".

KONIGSTEIN
(Sachsen)

Location
28, Km SE of DRESDEN.

Type
It was a KL until 1936/7, but in December 1943 it was reported as a PW camp with Army guards.
It is also a disciplinary camp for officers.

KONIGSWUSTERHAUSEN
(Brandenburg)

Location
27 Km. SE of BERLIN.

Type
A camp for Volksschädlinge (anti-social elements) including expelled SA, SS men and possibly military personnel.

Remarks
It is probably controlled by SACHSENHAUSEN.
SS Art. Schule 1 at GLAU bei TREBBIN, SW of BERLIN.
Kraftfahrzengamt at PAETZ.

KONITZ (CHOJNICE)
(Poland)

May be identical with ZAMARTE; not confirmed.

KONSTANTINOW

Near LITZMANNSTADT; also reported as KONSTANTYNOW.
Reported in September, 1941, as KL for priests and in March 1942, as transit camp for "expropriated Poles".
Recently again mentioned as KL.

KONSTANTYN I
(Poland)

Near LEMZA.
Transit camp.

KORINTH (CORINTH)
(Greece)

Peloponnes; KL established by the Germans.
Reported with 200 inmates June 1944.

KOSMINEK
(Poland)

Suburb of LUBLIN.
Forced Labour Camp.

KOSOVSKA MITROVICA
(Yugoslavia)
Near the river Sitnica.
Reported as a Gestapo prison camp, but may well be a KL.

KOSOW PODLASKI
(E Poland)
Reported in September 1942, as extermination camp for jews.

KRAKAU (KRAKOW)
Type.
Reported in November, 1942, as transit camp and in 1943 as "punitive camp for forced labour" controlling the following camps:-
DISTRICT LIBAN, LUBLICZ STRET (given as Nr. 2), KRAKAU PLASZOW, "CRACOW SUBURB", WOLA.DUCHNAKA. a forced labour camp.
Inmates
Estimate of inmates 5,000-8,000.
In HEIDELAGER, Post PUSTKOW über KRAKAU the following are located:-
Pi. Kp. der SS Kav. Div.
SS Estnisches Ausbildungs und Ersatz Bn.
SS Polizei Rgt. 23
SS Kradschützen Ersatz Abt.
SS Lazarett.
SS Pionier Ausbildungs und Ersatz Bn. 3
SS Kraftfahr Schule III
SS und Polizei Gericht.

KRAPJE
(Yugoslavia)
Croatia.
KL reported there, controlled by camp JASENOVAC.

KRASNIK
40 Km. SW of LUBLIN.
Type
May not be KL.
Inmates
Number of inmates estimated at 4,000.
Ghetto was established there.

KRETYNGA
(Lithuania)
Reported as KL for priests.

KROKEBERGSLETTA
(Norway)
Opened 1942
Inmates
Transferred there from SYDSPISSEN.
Estimated in January 1944, at 150-200.
Camp reported to be German operated.

KRONDORF	See EMSLAND.

KSANJIL
  (Bulgaria)	Thrace; said to be in operation.
2,000 inmates reported.

KUHBERG
  (Würtemberg)	Near Blaubeuren.
Last reported November 1937.

KULM (CHELMNO)
  (Poland)	64 Km. NE of LITZMANNSTADT; also called KULMHOF.
    Reported as KL for jews, priests and nuns and as extermination camp for jews.

KUTNO
  (Poland)	Near POSEN.
Telephone directory 1942 lists "Judenlager", Posner Strasse.

KVAENANGEN
  (Norway)	Near OSLO.

KVAM
  (Norway)	Location
    5 Km. from NORDHEIMSUND.
Type
    Camp is referred to as FRAMNES UNGDOMSKOLE ("Youth School"), possibly pre-invasion designation for the site.
Inmates
    Since June 1942, an internment camp for children and old people.
    Inmates capable of work were sent to Germany; inmates comparatively well off.
    A report of November 1943 speaks of 210 hostages there.
Guards.
    Norwegian Police guards and an NS Police man in charge.

L

LABLAU
(Ostpreussen)
Near KÖNIGSBERG. Reported before and after 1939.
KL; believed to be old Zuchthaus.
SS Units in the Vicinity.
SS und Polizei Gericht (KÖNIGSBERG)
Ergänzungsstelle der Waffen-SS (KÖNIGSBERG)

LAGER No. 21
(Hannover)
Near HANNOVER; 600 prisoners, with SS guards reported there in January, 1943.

LA LANDE A MONTS
(France, Indre-et-Loire)
Reported as internment camp; not confirmed as German or Vichy operated KL. May be detention camp of another type.

LAMIAS
See LIANOKLSDHI

LANDE
(France)
ANGERS region.
Reported as KL for women and communists.

LANDERNEAU
(France, Finistere)
Type
  In December, 1943, the STADIUM was reported as being prepared as KL in case of an Allied invasion.
Remarks
  Said to be surrounded by a 2-metre wall with 3-metre wire fence inside; wooden towers in SW and NE corners, with platform 4 metres high.

LANDSBERG/Lech
(Bayern)
Last reported, 1936. Fortress where HITLER was imprisoned.

LANGEN
(Hessen)
Probably in Land Hessen. Last reported, May, 1938; no details known.

LANGLUETGEN
(Hannover)
Near BREMEN. Last reported, 1936.

LARISSA
(Greece)
Thessaly.
Type
  KL established by the Italians in the old barracks of Larissa AA Bty.
Inmates
  August, 1943: 2,000 Jews, 2,000 Greek hostages and 1,500 Russians reported there, but July, 1944: only 84 persons were reported as confined there. (cont'd.)

LARISSA
  (Greece)(cont'd.)
Families of guerrillas detained there.
Personalities
  Capt. von HALDENWAND, commandant, July, 1944.

LARZAC
  (France, Dordogne)
25 miles WSW of BERGERAC.
An old airfield reported in July, 1943, as being used as camp for 200 Poles and Czechs.

LATHEN
  (Hannover)
See EMSLAND

LAUFEN/Salzach
  (Bayern)
Type
  Arbeitslager for women; referred to in German newspapers as KL.
  Sister institution to BERNAU am CHIEMSEE.
Inmates
  537 women in December, 1943, according to German source.
  800 in January, 1944.

LEMBERG (LWOW)
  (Poland)
In November, 1942, only one big transit camp at Janowska Street reported; in October, 1943, however, Lemberg camp was reported as identical with or in control of FRYDRYCHOWKA, a "punitive camp for forced labour"
LWOW II reported as permanent KL.
SS Troops in the Vicinity
Several companies of the SS Freiwilligendivision "Galizien" and SS Polizei Rgt. 24 are located there.
Truppenwirtschaftslager der Waffen-SS
SS Standort Verwaltung
SS Veterinär Untersuchungsamt.

LENES
  (Norway)
Near TROMSØ

LERCHENFLUR
  (Saarland)
Near SAARBRÜCKEN.
Probably not in operation.

LES ALLIERS
  (France, Charente)
Probably identical with and the correct name of ALLIERS.
198 men, women and children reported in August, 1943.

LES/MILES
(France, Bouches du Rhone)

Type
Not confirmed as German or Vichy operated KL. May be a detention camp of another type.
Capacity
An old brick factory with a capacity for 3,000-4,000 men.
Inmates
Germans, Austrians and Ex-Legionaries until 1940.
Then it became a transit camp for Jews and aliens.
September, 1943: inmates moved out. One report states that 1,400 inmates were kept at camp and new location is in Bordeaux region.
Guards
Old French Army men up to the end of the French campaign

LESCHWITZ
(Schlesien)

Near GOERLITZ.
Last reported in 1936.

LESLAU (WLOCLAWEK)
(Poland)

WARTHEGAU. Reported as KL. There is an SS Heimatpferdepark in LESLAU.

LEVADHIS (LEVADIA)
(Greece)

Attika Boeotia.
Type
KL, established by the Italians outside the town. Now under German control.
Inmates
1,500 reported, January, 1944.
Only 77 (hostages) in July, 1944.

LE VERDON
(France, Dordogne)

According to another source LE-VERDON-SUR-MER (Gironde).
Inmates are Jews convicted of fraud or sexual crimes.

LE VERNET
(France, Ariege)

In April, 1943: 1,800 inmates, mainly Jewish refugees reported there. Commissaire LUDEMAN in charge.

Also reported as being located in the Pyrenees Orientales, Montpellier region, with 1,000-1,500 political prisoners.

LIANOKISDHI (LIANOCLADI)
(Greece)

Phthiotis. KL reported with 150 inmates in February, 1944, but with only 80 inmates in July, 1944.

The LIBAN QUARRY
(Poland)

Near KRAKAU. Forced Labour Camp.
See also KRAKAU.

LICHTENBERG (Bayern)	Reported as LICHTENBURG, which does not exist; there is a LICHTENBERG near BAYREUTH. Reported to have been opened in 1938 for women only. Possibly identical with ANSBACH.
LICHTENBURG (Sachsen)	Near TORGAU. In operation in 1934, probably no longer in operation. **Inmates** 1,100 reported last (February, 1944). **Personalities** SCHMIDT: Commandant before 1936 BARANOWSKI: Commandant Jan.-Sep.1936 REMMERT: Deputy Jan.-Sep.1936 HELWIG: SBF, Commandant 1938 SCHMIDT: OSBF, reported Commandant.
LICHTERFELDE (Brandenburg)	Near EBERSWALDE. Last reported as KL in 1936. PW camp in February, 1944.
LIEBAU (Niederschlesien)	Regierungsbezirk Liegnitz. Work camp for Poles.
LIMBURG (Bayern)	Near ATTEL. Reported last as Russian PW camp (February, 1944).
LIMOGES (France, Haute Vienne)	Two new camps in the vicinity of LIMOGES were reported in November, 1943. Capacity 3,000. Type and status of camps not determined.
LIPNIK (Czechoslovakia)	Internment camp for next of kin of statesmen, politicians, government officials, etc. who escaped from German dominated territory. In 1943 relatives of Dr. BENES said to be interned here. **Remarks** No town by that name listed in 1940 directory for Böhmen-Mähren, only LIPNIC (LIPNISCH).
LITZMANNSTADT (LODZ) (Poland)	**Type** The following camps have been reported here in July, 1941:- (1) Transit camp for "expropriated Poles" (2) Correction camp for Polish youths (LODZ IV) (3) Experimental camp for the improvement of the Nordic race. (4) Concentration camp at RADOGOSZCZ (5) A "Dulag" at RADOGOSZCZ II. (cont'd.)

LITZMANNSTADT (LODZ)
  (Poland)(cont'd.)

The following have also been reported:-

LODZ I, a transit camp consisting of four camps
LODZ II, a permanent KL.
SS Units in the Vicinity

SS Röntgen-Sturmbann
SS Sanitätslager
Bekleidungslager der Waffen-SS
SS Einwanderungszentral.
Personalities
  Commandant is said to have been OSF Hans RONACHER. In view of the estimated figure of 35,000 inmates the command of RONACHER (a Lt.) seems unlikely to have been exercised over all these camps.

LOISSONS
  (France)

Aisne, Laon region. Reported recently; exact location unknown.

LOKEREN (LOCHERE)
  (East Flanders)

Is alleged to be an SK camp for members of the Wehrmacht, but may be a regular prison.

LOND
  (Poland)

9 Km. S of SLUPIEC on the Warta. A concentration camp for clergy reported there.

LOPUSZNO
  (Poland)

Near KIELCE. Reported in March, 1943, as punitive camp "for forced labour for peasants".

LUBLIN
  (Poland)

Type
  Lublin is said to control the following camps:-

KL at DZIESIATA
"Punitive camp for forced labour" at LUBLIN-KOSMINEK
KL for Jews in Lipowa-Street
"Dulag" at Krochmalna-Street
"Punitive camp for forced labour" near river Krzna.
  Telephone directory 1941 gives "Judisches Arbeitslager", Lindenstr.7
  One report refers to the KL at Lublin- assuming that there is only one- as "KL Lublin der Waffen-SS"
          (cont'd.)

LUBLIN
(Poland)(cont'd.)

Personalities
FUSS   HSF
FASSTEDT   HSF
FLORSTEDT   HSF
Richard TROMMER OSF

SS Units in the Vicinity

SS Polizei Rgt.13
SS Polizei Rgt.25
Hauptnachschublager der Waffen-SS
Kraftfahrzeugamt der Waffen-SS
SS Standort Kommandantur
SS Remonteamt (REJOWICE)
Kriegsgefangenenlager.

See also PONIATOW

LUKOW area
(Poland)

On the Krzna river. A forced labour camp is reported there.

LWOW

See LEMBERG

LYSKA
(W Poland)

Reported in October, 1943, as transit camp for "expropriated Poles".

M

MACAU
(France, Gironde)

KL for "labour evaders", reported in March, 1943

**MÄHRISCH OSTRAU
(MORAVSKA OSTRAVA)**
(Czechoslovakia)

Type
    Reported as camp for the area of Moravska Ostrava and Velke Kuncice (the latter name not in the directory for Böhmen Mähren).
Inmates
    In May, 1944, the inmates of this camp were reported to be working in the region N of Ostrau, probably doing clearing, grading, and rough construction work.

MAJDANEK
(Poland)

Near LUBLIN.
Reported in 1942 and 1943.
Type
    Mentioned variously as KL "Dulag", part of Doppellager AUSCHWITZ, and also as extermination camp.
    One report mentions three camps located there.

MAJDANEK, special concentration camp with enclosures for women.
MAJDANEK I, transit camp.
MAJDANEK II, KL and annihilation camp. (These are the camps referred to in the newspapers as "the LUBLIN extermination camps").
Inmates
    Unconfirmed estimates of number of inmates range from 25,000 to 50,000.

MALINES (MECHELEN)
(Belgium)

Inmates
    The Dossin barracks house Jewish inmates. In July, 1943, 1,200 of them left for unknown destination.
August, 1943: 450 were reported to be still there.
March, 1944: two trainloads of inmates from this camp were seen passing through HASSELT.
Guards
    1 officer, 4 NCOs and 24 Belgian SS men are reported to guard this camp.
Personalities
    Commandant Polizeimajor Dr. SCHMIDT is reported to have been in charge, from January, 1944, on.
An OSBF SCHMIDT is reported in BREENDONCK; same date.

A71

MALKINIA (NE Poland) — Reported in September, 1941, as "correctional camp".

MALOSZYCE (Poland) — Reported as KL.

MANNHEIM — See KÄFERTAL.

MANTUA (Italy) — No details.

MANZAC (France) — Limoges region.
Type
A three section camp for Communists, Gaullists and Jews.

MARBURG/Drau (MARIBOR) (Yugoslavia) —
Type
The MEHLINGER barracks are the main KL area, separated by a wire fence from the PW Camp.
Inmates
800 - 1,000, Jews from ZAGREB, priests, doctors, lawyers, mayors, etc.
Remarks
It is reported that inmates were shot for looking out of windows, had to stand at attention in presence of guards, etc.
SS Units in the Vicinity
SS Röntgen Sturmbann at Krieuubergasse 31.

MARSEILLE (France, Bouches-du-Rhone) — According to a report dated February, 1943, FORT ST. NICOLAS was "taken over by the Germans" in November, 1942.
Inmates
In January, 1943, Polish internees were reported at the "German controlled" FORT ST. PIERRE. BRABAN, in this area, is a "transit camp for aliens"; capacity about 1,000.

MATHILDEN-SCHLÖSSCHEN (Sachsen) — Near DRESDEN.
Last reported in existence in May, 1938.

MAUTHAUSEN (Oberdonau) — 19 Km. SE of LINZ.
Consists of three camps:- MAUTHAUSEN (controlling all three), GUSEN and ST. GEORGEN. (Cont'd.)

MATHAUSEN
  (Oberdonau)
  (cont'd.)

Total Inmates (three camps).
   Estimated by local population at about 20,000; reported to be Spanish loyalists, unreliable Germans, work evaders, Jews, sentenced criminals, homosexuals, Poles, Czechs and other foreigners. Inmates work at quarries on the Danube electricity works, at the Hermann Göring works near LINZ, and on building construction. Inmates wear blue and white striped overalls, and a round brimless cap. Heads cut close with a stripe almost shaved through the centre.

Guards
   Waffen SS, according to a report of March 1944. Outside the camp they are posted at intervals of 50 metres.
   Inside guards said to be Waffen SS and Werkschutz, mostly older retired men of the Steyr works (where a small branch of the KL, about 200 men, is working, at the Walzwerk). The Werkschutz wear a grey-blue uniform, with a combination of chevrons and pips.

SS Units in the Vicinity
   SS Totenkopfstandarte "Ostmark" (original home station VIENNA), may have elements nearby. (See "Personalities").

Details of MAUTHAUSEN Camp
   Mentioned as KL in German telephone directory. Continuously in operation; partly burned down, but may have been restored.
   Consisted in April, 1942, of 20 blocks of dwelling houses, plus underground prison cells.
   About 6,000 inmates reported in 1940; they are largely Jews, some of whom are especially brought here for gas experiments.

Details of GUSEN and ST. GEORGEN Camps
   Almost adjacent to MAUTHAUSEN, all three being within 5 km. of each other.
   GUSEN was also reported in 1944 as a "twin" camp, GUSEN-ST. GEORGEN.
   East of ST. GEORGEN-GUSEN is ST. GEORGEN-LAGERSTEIN, also reported as an internment camp.
   GUSEN said to have been a KL for priests in September, 1941, and for Spaniards in April, 1942.

Personalities

ZEEREIS	OSBF Commandant in 1940 and 1942, probably continuously.
Dr. Eduard KREBSBACH	SBF Garrison M.O.
QUIRZFELD	SS SBF Commander SS Totenkopf Stand. "Ostmark."
SAND	OSF Chief Administrative Officer
Bruno KITT	USF

MAUZAC
(France, Correze)
Camp for "communists, Gaullists and Jews". Also for Loyalist Spaniards. Possibly a double camp.

MEINSDORF
(Brandenburg)
Near JÜTERBOG.
Last reported in 1936.

MELSUNGEN
See KASSEL-MELSUNGEN.

MERIGNAC
(France, Gironde)
A camp BEAU-DESERT-MERIGNAC has been reported but is probably a mistake for the BEAU-DESERT camp in PICHEY. A German police school is located in MERIGNAC.

METZ
(France, Lorraine)
Reported as "one of five French camps for Jews", but not confirmed.
SS Units in the Vicinity
   SS Nachrichten Ausb. Abt. 4 (MÖRCHINGEN).
   SS Nachrichten Schule.
   Truppenwirtschaftslager der Waffen SS (MÖRCHINGEN)
   SS Remonteamt (PELTERS)
   SS und Polizeigericht
   SS Lazarett (PELTERS)
   Kurierstelle der Waffen SS

MICHENDORF
(Yugoslavia)
KL reported there.

MIECHELSGESTEL
See St. MIECHELSGESTEL

MIECHOW
(Poland)
35 Km. N. of Krakau.
Possibly not a KL but may be identical with ghetto located there.

MIEDNIEWICE
(Poland)
Near LOWICZ.
Reported in January, 1942, as "hard labour camp for peasants".

NIEDZYCHOD
See BIRNBAUM.

MILOWITZ
(MILOWICE)
(Czechoslovakia)
Location
   Near Prague
Type
   Confirmed as KL at the end of 1943.
SS Units in the Vicinity

   SS Artillerie Schule 2 (PRAG-BENESCHAU).
   SS Truppen-Übungs-Platz "BÖHMEN" (PRAG-BENESCHAU).
   SS Panzer Grenadier Ausbildungs und Ersatz Btl. 2. (PRAG-RUSIN)
(Cont'd.)

MILOWITZ
(MILOVICE)
(Czechoslovakia)
(Cont'd.)

SS Ausbildungs Regt. z.b. V.
SS Polizei Grenadier Regt. (BENESCHAU).
SS Reit-und Fahrschule II.
SS Artillerie Ausbildungs und Ersatz Regt. (SELTSCHAN near PRAG).
SS Pionier Ausbildung und Ersatz Bn. 2. (PIKOWITZ, near PRAG).
Komp. SS Panzer Spähwagen Ersatz Bn. (BUKOWAN, near PRAG).
SS Fallschirmjäger Ersatz Komp. (CHLUM, near PRAG).
SS Panzer Ausbildungs und Ersatz Regt. (BENESCHAU).
SS Pionier Schule (BENESCHAU).
SS Pionier Schule (DAWLE, near PRAG).
SS Pionier Schule (RADISCHKO, near PRAG).
SS Sturm Geschütz Schule, (BUKOWAN, near PRAG).
SS Sturm Geschütz Schule B (JANOWITZ, near PRAG).
SS Kavallerie Truppen Übungsplatz (JUSTINITZ, near PRAG).
SS Junkerschule (PRAG-DEVITZ).
SS Sanitätschule (PRAG).
Truppenwirtschaftslager der Waffen-SS. (BENESCHAU).
Hauptzeugamt der Waffen SS (PRAG).
Kraftfahrzeugamt der Waffen SS (PRAG).
SS Sanitätszweiglager (PRAG).
SS Kleiderkasse (PRAG).
SS Wachebataillon (PRAG).
SS Standortverwaltung (PRAG).
Ergänzungstelle der Waffen SS (Nebenstelle BÖHMEN und MÄHREN, at PRAG IV, Czerninpalais).
SS und Polizeigericht (PRAG)
SS Fürsorge und Versorgungsamt Ausland (PRAG II, Karl Laznovskyufer 60).
SS Lazarett (PRAG).

MIRANDA
(France, Gers)

Not confirmed. There is a camp MIRANDA DE EBRO in Spain in which political refugees of various nations were detained.

Inmates

Of the 1,700 Frenchmen reported in November, 1943, the majority had fled from forced labour in Germany. They were transferred to Africa in groups of 100 to 300.

The communist inmates were mostly Germans.

A release from this camp could be obtained by those who could produce a visa for another country.

MLOCINY
(Poland)
: Near WARSAW.
Reported in February, 1943, as a recently established KL.

MOERDIJK
(Holland, Noord-Brabant).
: For political prisoners and Jews.
See also VUGHT.

MONT-DE-MARSAN
(France, Landes)
: Reported February, 1943.
Reported as internment camp for "people who attempted to escape over the Pyrenees".
Possibly identical with LA LANDE A MONTS.

MOORLAGER
(Hannover)
: See EMSLAND.
(Colloquial name for ESTERWEGEN and other camps of group EMSLAND).

MORINGEN
(Hannover)
: **Location**
18 Km. N of GÖTTINGEN.
Type
Reported in 1933 - 34 as KL for men and women (Political prisoners) and subsequently for women only.
Inmates
800 women inmates were reported there. In 1938 the women inmates were transferred to GROSSROSEN.
After 1941 the camp was either partly or entirely transformed into a Jugendschutzlager der Sipo (Security police camp for the protective custoday of boys).

MÜHLHEIM
(Rheinland)
: Near DUISBURG.
Last reported in 1936.

MÜNSTERBERG
(Schlesien)
: 57 Km. S of BRESLAU. Last reported in May, 1938 and probably no longer in operation.

MYROS IRAKLION
: See AGIOS MYRON

MYSLOWICE
(Poland)
: **Type**
Reported in September, 1942 as a transit camp with an especially large section for women.
It may be identical with the camp which has been reported as:

MYSLOWICE II A "Special KL with enclosures for women". (Cont'd).

MYSLOWICE
(Poland)
(Cont'd.)

October, 1942: Reported as "a punitive camp for forced labour".
March, 1943: inmates estimated that 3,000 Poles were held there.
January, 1944: reported to have 1,000 inmates.

Remarks
    A considerable number of inmates had died from typhus, according to report.

MYTILENE
(Greece)

Aegean. KL reported as run by Germans at DIDOSTXDION.

N

NAKEL   See POTULITZ.

NASIELSK
(N Poland)   60 Km north of WARSAW.

NATZWEILER
(France, Alsace)   Highest mortality rate of all camps except extermination camps.

May be identical or affiliated with SCHIRMECK.

Inmates
    March 1942: 930 inmates
    August 1942: 540 inmates. The decrease was "not the result of release."
    1943: Number of inmates increased again to over 1,000.

Work
    Interior duties (laundry, etc.)
    Construction and quarry work, using about 200 men each.

Remarks
    The quarry belongs to the <u>Deutsche Erd- und Steinbruchwerke SS Neubauleitung Deutschland Reichsführung Berlin</u> (an SS enterprise).

Motor cars, lorries, and other vehicles have number 12,000 - 12,500.

Private cars of officers have civilian plates of the MOLSHEIM district.

Personalities in 1942

RÖDL	OSF	probably commandant before 1942; later in AUSCHWITZ with rank of OSBF.
Egon ZILL	SBF	reported after 1942 in FLOSSENBURG.
KRAMMER	OSF	1. Lagerführer; probably still there.
HINKELMANN	OSF	2. Lagerführer
FASCHING-BAUR	OSF	
SCHLACHTER	OSF	
Dr. EISELE	OSF	M.O. "notorious killer." formerly at BUCHENWALD.
STRASSER	Oschaf	in charge of motor pool.
HACKER	Oschaf	1. Kasernenführer
WITZIG	Schaf	in charge of quarry.
Ernst ROHRSCHACH		Lagerältester (a prisoner)
KASEBERG		In charge of Strafkdo (punitive detail); a prisoner.

NAUPLIA
    (Greece)   Unconfirmed.

NAXOS (Island of)
    (Greece)   In the Cyclades. Unconfirmed report of KL there.

NEUBERSDORF   See NIEBOROWITZ

NEUENGAMME   See HAMBURG NEUENGAMME

NEURRANDENBURG-
   KÖNIGSWUSTERHAUSEN   See KÖNIGSWUSTERHAUSEN

NEUSTADT
    (Bayern)   Last reported in 1936.

NEUSUSTRUM   See EMSLAND.

NEXON
    (France, Haute Vienne)   August, 1943: 400 "labour evaders" Gaullists, and Jews" were detained here.

NIEBOROWITZ
(NIEBEROWICE)
    (Schlesien)   Near GLEIWITZ. Renamed NEUBERSDORF. Reported as KL for Russian PW.

NIEDERHAGEN
    (Mecklenburg)   Near ROSTOCK. Believed to be in operation.
Personalities
    Adolf HAAS   HSF Commandant
    Heinrich   OSF Deputy
    GRUETER   Commandant.
    MICHL   OSF Leiter der Lagerverwaltung.
    Dr. METZGER   OSF Senior Camp MO.
    Dr. Gerhard
    KRIEGER   SBF Garrison MO.

NISH
    (Yugoslavia)   Serbia. KL reported in the vicinity.

NOE
    (France Haute Garonne)   Status of camp not determined. September 1941: 1,3000 aliens. reported interned there.

NORDMO
    (Norway)   Near SVANIK.

O

OBENRODE (Hessen) — Near DARMSTADT. Believed to be in operation.

OBERGRUPPE (GORNA GRUPA) (Poland) — Near GRAUDENZ. Located near a Truppenübungsplatz. Reported as a segregation and transit camp.

OBERLANGEN/Ems — See EMSLAND

OBRA (W Poland) — Either 7 Km. S of JAROTSCHIN or 7 Km. SW of WOLLSTEIN. Definitely in W Poland.
Reported as KL for priests. Probably not in operation since 1940.

ORTUMSAND — Near OLDENBURG but location not found. Directory has only ORTUM. Last reported in 1936.

ODERBERG (S Poland) — Polish BOGUMIN
Czech BOHUMIN

October, 1943: reported as segregation camp for "expropriated Poles".

ØSTERDALEN (Norway) — Several camps reported in that province one of which was certain to exist in 1941.

OHRDRUF (Thüringen) — Reported prior to 1939. Not confirmed. Although it is believed to be a women's camp it may be a KL or Militärstraflager. Army schools and establishments in the vicinity.

OMMEN (Holland) — Camp. Nat. Jeugdstorm. Referred to as the "Erica" forced labour camp.
Capacity
  2,000
Type
  Probably for black marketeers. Possibly also for Berufsverbrecher (Habitual criminals).

OLYMPISCHES DORF (Brandenburg) — Near BERLIN. Last reported in April, 1943. 6,000 inmates.

OPAWA — See TROPPAU

O

ORANIENBURG See SACHSENHAUSEN.

ORLEANS
(France, Loiret) Not confirmed as German or Vichy operated KL. May be a detention camp of another type.

ORTENSTEIN
(Sachsen) Near Zittau. Last reported in 1936. There is an SS.Lazarett in SENNERSDORF bei ZITTAU.

OSLO
(Norway)
Type
The AKERSHUS prison, the largest in Norway, is said to have been used recently as transit camp for political prisoners who are to be transported to Germany.
SS Units stationed in the vicinity.
Truppenwirtschaftslager der Waffen SS
SS Wachbataillon 6
SS und Polizeigericht
Ersatz inspektion der Waffen SS
(Drammensveyen 105 and Nobelsgt 10)
SS Standorthommandantur
SS Röntgen-Sturmbann

OSNABRÜCK
(Hannover) At OSNABRÜCK. Last reported in 1936.

OSTERSTEIN Possibly in Sachsen or Thüringen. confirmed as existing under that name in 1942. Reported near Kirchberg in May, 1938.

OSTHOFEN
(Hessen) Possibly 34 Km. S of MAINZ. Reported before 1939. Not confirmed.

OSTLAND
(Lithuania) Possibly identical with RIGA. Believed to be in operation.

OSTROW (OSTROWO)
(Poland)
Type
Reported in 1943 as "punitive camp for forced labour". Controls branch in PLESCHEN.
Remarks
SS Arbeitsstab at Kirchplatz, PROLSTRI.

OSWIECIM See AUSCHWITZ.

OUDLEUSDEN
(Holland)
Location
2 miles S of AMERSFOORT.

O

OUDLEUSDEN (Contd.)

Inmates
July, 1943: 5,000 "political prisoners" reported here.
Other sources report this camp to be SS controlled and primarily for Jews.

See also AMERSFOOT.

P

PABIANITZ (PABIANICE) (Poland)
Near LITZMANNSTADT.
Reported in 1939/40 as "Dulag" with approximately 15,000 inmates.
Reported in February, 1941, as "Dulag for priests and Jews".

PALVOS MELSS
See SALONIKA.

PAPENBURG (Hannover)
Headquarters of group of camps known as EMSLAND.
Personalities
    Commandant of entire group believed to be SA-OF Regierungsdirektor Dr. SCHÄFER, who is also reported as commandant of SA-Standarte "EMSLAND".
    SA-OSF KELM and SA-Stuf BLOCK may also be at this HQ or at one of the subordinate camps.
    Regierungsrat SCHERMER and Regierungsrat BAUMERT are also reported to be at this HQ.
    Lt. SCHAFER is Police Chief in Papenburg (town) but not believed to be connected with the camp's administration.

For camp at PAPENBURG see also EMSLAND.

PARIS (France)
CHERCHE MIDI prison and VELODROME D'HIVER have been used for political prisoners of Paris region and also for escapees from OT.
    PARIS may also be the seat of the controlling HQ of DRANCY, FRESNES, and FORT DE ROMAINVILLE. SEE DRANCY and FRESNES. No further reports on the last named camp.
    The PARC DES PRINCES Camp is used for Jewish inmates.
    The PETITE ROQUETTE prison is also reported as a concentration camp.
SS Units in the Vicinity
Truppenwirtschaftslager der Waffen-SS (PARIS-VILLETTES)
Ersatzkommando der Waffen-SS (24 Ave. Raymond Poincaré)
SS und Polizei Gericht (PARIS)
Kurierstelle der Waffen-SS (PARIS)

PAROI (Greece)
KL reported to be in the vicinity.

PATRAS (Greece)	Peloponnese. KL established by Italians and probably situated in town prisons. Reported in May 1944 with 170 inmates. Now under German control.
PAU (France, Basses Pyrenees)	September 1942, "many Poles" were reported there, at the PELOTTA Stadium.
PAULO MELAS barracks (Greece)	Salonika area. No details on hand.
PAVLON MELA THESSALONIKA	See SALONIKA.
PAXOI (Greece)	Ionian Islands, near Corfu. KL established by the Italians.
PELNINIA (Poland)	Reported as KL for Jews and Poles. KL for Jews has been reported as Polkinia III.
PETITE ROQUETTE	See PARIS.
PETRASIULA (Lithuania)	Suburb of KAUNUS. Details unknown
PICHEY (France, Gironde)	The BEAU-DESERT camp reported as KL. "Black marketeers, labour evaders, Jews and communists" reported as inmates in October, 1943.
PIEKOSZOW	See KIELCE.
PILSEN (PLZEN) (Czechoslovakia)	Confirmed up to November, 1943. "Wiesengrund" mental hospital used for Czech intellectuals; all sterilised, no releases.
PIONKI (Poland)	Near RADOM. Reported in June, 1943, as "punitive camp for forced labour".
PITHIVIERS (France, Loiret)	Reported as internment camp, not as KL. In October, 1943, 650 communists and Jews were interned here. A doctor is said to have resigned because of poor conditions in this camp.

PLANNINA (Greece)	KL reported in vicinity.
PLASOW	See KRAKAU.
PLESCHEN (PLESZEW) (Poland)	N of OSTROW; reported in January, 1943, as branch of punitive camp OSTROW.
PLESKAU (Russia)	Believed to be in operation.
PLESZEW	See PLESCHEN.
PLOEHNEN (PLONSK) (Poland)	58 Km. N of WARSAW; reported as KL.
PLONSK	See PLOEHNEN.
PLZEN	See PILSEN.
PLOCK	See SCHRÖTTERSBURG.
POITIERS (France, Vienne)	Former PW camp near airdrome was pre-selected to become KL in case of Allies landing. 200 Jews and Gypsies reported there in June, 1943.
POMIECHOWEK (Poland)	Transit Camp. Railway stop north of Warsaw. 3 Km. north of Nowy Dwor.
POMIECHOWEK I (Poland)	North of Warsaw. Permanent KL.
POMIECHOWEK II (Poland)	North of Warsaw. KL for Jews.
PONTIVY (France)	SK-Lager, reported as being primarily for OT personnel.
PONIATOW (Poland)	Near LUBLIN. In July, 1943, it was reported as a "punitive camp for forced labour and Jews". It was mentioned in one report as LUBLIN-PONIATOW, an establishment consisting of 4 camps with 4,000 inmates at PONIATOW proper and a total of 14,000. (This figure may include other LUBLIN camps.)

POSEN (POZNAN) (Poland)
: **Type**
Reported in 1939/40 as a "Dulag" with 15,000 inmates.
Other Camps
Possibly identical with the above are:

GLOWNA-STREET, a "Dulag" reported in July, 1942.
Fort VII a, reported as a KL, but may be identical with POSEN-TRESKAU.
PUSZYKOW and ZABIKOW may also be administered by POSEN.
SS Units in the Vicinity
SS und Polizei Gericht
Ergänzungsstelle der Waffen-SS (Königsring 22)
SS Röntgen Sturmbann.

POSEN-TRESKAU (Poland)
: Small KL there since Junkerschule "BRAUNSCHWEIG" was transferred there, replacing the SS Unterführerschule. Possibly identical with FORT VII a.

POTULITZ (POTULICE) (Poland)
: Near NAKEL, 20 Km. west of Bromberg. Also referred to as NAKEL.
Type
Reported in March 1942 as punitive camp for Poles refusing to enlist as Volksdeutsche.
November, 1942, reported as transit camp for "expropriated Poles".
December, 1943, reported as KL and forced labour camp for 15,000.
Inmates
September, 1942, 4,000 inmates.
October, 1943, 3,000 Poles reported there.
Remarks
May be identical with POTULITZ II which has been reported as KL for Jews.

POZNAN
: See POSEN.

PREUSSISCH STARGARD (STAROGARD) (Poland)
: 40 Km. SSW of DANZIG.
Reported once as "possibly for Jews only".
Reported in March, 1942, as "punitive camp for forced labour" for Poles refusing to enlist as Volksdeutsche.

PROWENISZKI (Lithuania)
: Near KAUNAS; reported in September, 1943, as KL "for Polish priests of the VILNA district."

PRZEDZIELNICA (SE Poland)
: Near PRZEMSYL; reported in October, 1943, as "punitive camp for forced labour".

PUCK   See PUTZIG.

PUSTKOW   10 km. NE of DEBICA.   Forced labour Camp.
    (Poland)

PUSZCZYKOW   Near POSEN.
    (W Poland)   Reported in 1939/40 as concentration camp
                       "for Polish priests".
                       Probably not in operation since summer,
                       1940.

R

RAB, Island of (ARBE)
(Italy)
Off the Dalmatian coast E of POLA. "For Jews".

RADOGOSZCZ
(Poland)
Suburb of LITZMANNSTADT. Reported as KL.

RADOM
(Central Poland)
Type
Report of June, 1943, claims over 8,000 Polish youths to be in "punitive camp for forced labour" in this district.
SS Units in the Vicinity

SS Veterinär Ersatz Abteilung
SS Lazarett
SS Pferdelazarett
SS Totenkopfschule

RADZIWILISZKI
(NE Poland)
In February, 1943, "punitive camp for forced labour" reported here.

RADZYMIN
(Poland)
Near WARSAW. Reported in August, 1941, as KL.

RAJSKO
(Poland)
Near AUSCHWITZ. Reported as KL. At one time AUSCHWITZ and RAJSKO together were reported to have 50,000 inmates, 20,000 of whom were Polish women.

RAUA RUSKA
(Poland)
NW of LEMBERG. Reported as KL for Jews.

RASTATT
(Baden)
SW of KARLSRUHE. Continued as KL up to 1938.
Hauptwirtschaftslage of the SS there.

RAVENSBRÜCK
(Mecklenberg)
Near FÜRSTENBERG
Type
Reported in November, 1941, as KL for women.
According to a report of July, 1944, there is a Jugendschutzlager der Sipo (Security Police camp for protective custody) for girls either close to or identical with the camp.
Inmates
Around 8,000, aged 16-60, "wives of Germans who fled, saboteurs, communists", etc. 500 Polish women reported there in December, 1943.
(cont'd.)

RAVENSBRÜCK (Mecklenburg) (cont'd.)	**Remarks** May be identical with FÜRSTENBERG, FÜRSTENBURG, and UCKERMARK. **SS Units in the Vicinity** An SS Nachschublager is established in RAVENSBRÜCK A Bauleitung der Bauinspektion Reich "Nord" of the Waffen-SS is located here. SS Bekleidungslager.
RECEBEDOU (France, Haute Garonne)	Near TOULOUSE. Rue St. Michel jail reported to be used for "terrorists".
REICHENBACH (Probably Schlesien)	50 Km. SW of BRESLAU, or may be in Sachsen near ZWICKAU. In operation in 1933. Reported in 1936 and again in 1938. Reported as a transit camp but probably no longer in operation. Possibly a PW camp now.
REMBERTOW (Poland)	Near WARSAW. Reported in January, 1943, as KL. Also reported as a forced labour camp, but both may exist.
RENDSBURG (Holstein)	Near KIEL. 400 Norwegian prisoners last reported in December, 1943.
RICKLING (Mecklenburg)	13 Km. SE of NEUMÜNSTER. Reported before 1939. Not confirmed.
RIEUCROS (France, Ariege)	Not confirmed as German or Vichy operated KL. May be detention camp of another type. Inmates: "women, mostly Jewish".
RIGA (Lithuania)	Possibly identical with OSTLAND. Believed to be in operation. **SS Units in the Vicinity** SS Lazarett SS Panzer Ausbildungs- und Ersatz- Regt. LETTLAND (?) SS Sanitätsschule (RIGA-ROTHENBERG) Truppenwirtschaftslager der Waffen-SS Bekleidungslager der Waffen-SS SS und Polizei Gericht SS Feldpostprüfung: Zweigstelle OSTLAND.

RIPPIN (RYPIN)   58 Km. NW of BRELAU, just over Polish
    (Poland)   border. Reported in 1939-1940 as
                          "KL for Polish priests" and as
                          "transit camp".

RIVESALTES   September, 1941: about "6,000 aliens"
    (France, Pyrenees   reported there. An unconfirmed
    Orientales)   report of October, 1942, estimates
                          the capacity of the camp to be
                          50,000.

RÖDELHEIM   Near FRANKFURT/Main. Reported
    (Hessen-Nassau)   before 1939.

ROSSLAU   6 Km. N of DESSAU. Reported as
    (Magdeburg-Anhalt)   having been women's camp only. Was
                          closed in 1938, but mentioned as
                          being in operation again in 1943,
                          possibly only for women.

ROUILLE   Type
    (France, Vienne)   Not confirmed as German or Vichy
                          operated KL; may be camp of another
                          type.
                          Inmates
                             In June, 1943, about 300 inmates
                          here; "black marketeers, political
                          prisoners, offenders against common
                          law".

RUDNIKI   10 Km. NE of TSCHENSTOCHAU. Reported
    (NE Poland)   in October, 1943, as "punitive camp
                          for forced labour".

RYBNIK   Reported in October, 1943, as transit
    (W Poland)   camp for "expropriated" Poles.

RYKOSZ   See KIELCE

RYPIN   See RIPPIN

                                    S

SAARLAUTERN   Reported as KL for "Russian women".
    (Saarland)

SACHSENBURG   14 Km. NE of Chemnitz.
    (Sachsen, Flöhn)   Identified in 1933; probably no longer
                          in operation.
                          1500 prisoners in 1938.
                          Personalities
                             Lagerkommandant Rödel, 1936.

SACHSENHAUSEN
(Brandenburg)

30 Km. north of BERLIN.
Name of one of the largest KL's.
Really 2 camps, 1) SACHSENHAUSEN
              2) ORANIENBURG
Both near the town of ORANIENBURG.
Little information is available on the Oranienburg camp which was closed for a time and opened again in 1941. It was reported to have 3,000 inmates, in August 1943.
The following information therefore concerns SACHSENHAUSEN only.

Type

Between 1938 and 1941 the camp consisted of:
1) Prisoner's camp
2) Commandant's camp
3) Deutsche Ausrüstungswerke (an SS enterprise)
4) Camp for SS-Totenkopf-Standarte
5) SS settlement colony
6) Brick works

A large boot factory was established in the camp in 1940, but was not yet in operation in January, 1941.

The camp was so big that 21 Lagerführer each with an Arbeitsdienstführer, were said to exist. (See text, para 6.)

The prisoner's camp had 85 wooden buildings.

The Kommandanturlager was separated by a 10-foot wall above which electrically-charged wire was strung.

The SS-TV-Standarte had 15 barracks for 150 men each, 8 other two-storey barracks and 6 three-storey brick barracks.

For Polish inmates there was the "Holenlarger" also known as "Quarantine" where especially harsh treatment was meted out.

Six isolated barracks were reserved for the Strafkompagnie.

Inmates

April 1940. 10,000 internees were said to be in this camp. These were:

1,000 Jews
1,500 Czechs (2/3 of them students)
500 Poles
7,000 Germans of whom 3,000 were classified as politically dangerous, and 4,000 as anti-social elements including habitual criminals.

May 1940: 4,000 Poles arrived here.
In the winter 1940/41 2,000 inmates are said to have died.

SACHSENHAUSEN (contd.) October 1941. A few barracks were segregated for Russian PWs.
Winter 1941/42: typhus became rampant bringing the total of deaths for the preceding two year period up to 12,000.
March 1942: 300 Jews were shot and the rest were removed from the camp.
April 1942: 120 Dutch officers were shot.
May 1942: at least 5,000 sick and crippled inmates were executed in so-called S-Kommandos.
August 1942: injection experiments began on Russians and Jews, the latter being specially imported from AUSCHWITZ.

December 1943: reported to have 25,000 inmates.

Inmates who tried to escape once are marked as "targets" by a red rosette on a white ground.
The number of inmates varies, but in 1941 their allocation for work was approximately as follows:

2,000 for construction of brick works
1,800 for Deutsche Ausrüstungswerke (D.A.W.)
800 in various shops for camp necessities
1,000 building SS Barracks
200 working on road construction
200 building A&P shelters (punishment squads)
40 at railroad station loading materials
300 working at new boot factory
600 working at clay quarry (mainly homosexuals expelled from the Party or SS)
50 digging out unexploded bombs aroung Berlin.

The rest as clerks, garage mechanics, crematorium attendants, etc.
Occasionally details of about 300 men were sent to work at the Heinkel Werke aerodrome at ORANIENBURG. These work a 14-hour day, but had better treatment.
The D.A.W. manufactures materials needed by the SS, such as furniture, electrical equipment etc.

SS Troops in the Vicinity

An SS-Erziehungssturm (believed to be a disciplinary company).
The following SS establishments, units, Ersatz units or elements thereof are located near the camps, and make use of local prison labour:

3/SS Totenkopf Wachbtl. Schutzkommando in ORANIENBURG (?)
SS Zentralzulassungsstelle ORANIENBURG

SACHSENHAUSEN (contd.) SS Hauptzeugamt ORANIENBURG
SS Kraftfahrzeugdepot ORANIENBURG
SS Nachrichtenzeugamt ORANIENBURG
SS Totenkopfstandarte BRANDENBURG
 (originally SS Totenkopf Sturmbann V
 "BRANDENBURG", Cmdr. SS SF NOSTITZ?)
SS Sanitäts Ersatz Bn. 2
SS Totenkopfstandarte "ORANIENBURG"
Elements of TV Regiment 10
SS Lehrküche
Secret Radio Station reported as bearing
the code name "Ace of Hearts" (Herz As)
SACHSENHAUSEN
Truppen Verwaltungsamt der SS-TV in
ORANIENBURG
Bauleitung der Waffen-SS und Polizei
ORANIENBURG
Zentralnachweis der Waffen-SS
SS Panzer Inst. Ausbildung und Ersatz Abt.
SS Dolmetsche Ausbildungs und Ersatz
Kompagnie Desinfektorenschule
Bekleidungslager
Bekleidungswerk der Waffen-SS
Storage warehouses of the Wirtschaftw-
verwaltungs- Hauptamt SACHSENHAUSEN
Kraftfahrtechnische Versuchsabteilung
der Waffen-SS
Lehr und Versuchsabteilung für das
Diensthundewesen der Waffen-SS
ORANIENBURG.

The Bauinspektion "Reich Nord" of the Waffen-SS and Police in Berlin used Oranienburg labour.

Of the 2,000 men in the Totenkopfstandarte 4 - 500 were permanently stationed in the camp while the others received training there, and were sent to the Eastern front as replacements arrived.

Personalities at KL, SACHSENHAUSEN

(a) Former camp commandants include:-

BARANOWSKI, Hermann	SSOF	Now dead
EICKE, Theodor	OGF	Now dead; see text para 5
EISFELD	OSBF	
LORENZ	SSOF	1940-42

(b) Latest reported personalities:-

KOLB	HSF	Camp Commandant reported removed (questionable source, July 1944)
GRIMM	OSF	Adj. (?)
HEIDRICH (?)	SS HSF	Deputy Commandant

SACHSENHAUSEN (contd.)

WEYMANN, Hans	HSF	
BÜTTNER	SS OSF	Formerly in charge of DAW office, Berlin
REHN	OSF	"In charge of prisoner's working parties"
VOLK		"Gestapo Chief" (possibly <u>Kommissar</u>) reported removed (as KOLB above)
CORNELLI	OS	
v. TODDEN	Krim. Sekr.	Gestapo
FORSTER	SS HSF	Reported there in 1941
LAVER	SS SBF	
KAINDL	SS OSBF	
BÖHM, Wilhelm		Foreman of crematorium and burial squad
SCHITLI		Rapportführer (later Blockführer)

(c) Undated personalities:-

CAMPE	Ustuf	
NOWACKI	Oschaf	
SORGE, known as Eiserner Gustav	Oschaf	
SCHUBERT	Oschaf	
FICKERT (or FIGGERT)	Oschaf	
BOGDALA	Oschaf	
SEIFERT	Oschaf	
GRÜNEWALD	SBF	Lagerführer
BRUM	Ustuf	Leader of the Administrative Coy under LORENZ
GENSIOR	Ustuf	Bauleiterführer
KILINGER	HSF	
SUREN	HSF	GRÜNEWALD's predecessor as Lagerführer
KLINGER	HSF	
SORGER (Bauleiter)	USF	)
RADICKE	Oschaf	) at SACHSENHAUSEN
LEHMANN	Uschaf	)
HOFFMANN, R.		)
BRAUN		)
SOMMER		) all SS men
BUGDALLE		)
KNITTEL		)
KAMPE		)

SACHSENHAUSEN (contd.)   **Personalities in ORANIENBURG (town), or in the vicinity of KL, SACHSENHAUSEN**

(a) Nachrichtenzeugamt:-

MATTIAT	SBF	Comd
NEUMANN	HSF	Ia
UROW	HSF	Comd of the workshops
SCHREIBER	HSF	Formerly responsible for accounts now posted
MZIK	HSF	Legal officer
EWERT	OSF	Formerly Adj., now at the SS Signal School in METZ
GREVER	OSF	FORMER Comd. of the districts, now posted
BAYER	OSF	Adj.
BÜCKER	OSF	Admin. officer
GILDNER	USF	Responsible for the constructional office and for the fitting of trucks to carry signals equipment, also connected with experimental unit
DIENSE	USF	Comd. of NZA districts
MAYER	USF	Admin. officer of the districts

(b) Bauleitung:-

SCHMÖLL	OSF	Comd.
HÖHLINGER	OSF	2 i/c

(c) Garrison, and local units

REUTTER, Dr.	SS HSF	Garrison M.O.
KAINDEL	SBF	Garrison Comd.
ZIERSCH	OSF	Garrison HQ (Had a house built for himself in ORANIENBURG, with official labour and material)
PIETSCH	HSF	Comd. of Garrison Adm.
SCHRIMM	OSF	2 i/c of Garrison Adm.
NOSTITZ	SS SF	Possibly comd. of TV-standarte BRANDENBURG
v. JENA	SSGF	Comd. of TV-standarte ORANIENBURG

SAETERMØN (Norway)   Reported as "small camp".

SAHRA (Hessen-Nassau)   Near KASSEL: believed to consist of 2 camps. Its existence was confirmed in 1941

ST. CYPRIEN (France)	Pyrenees Orientales or Dordogne. Status of camp not ascertained. Reported in June, 1943 to house a large number of "Jews and black marketeers".
ST. ETIENNE (France, Loire)	In December, 1942 1,000 political prisoners were reported there.
ST. GERMAIN LES BELLES (France, Haute Vienne)	300 "Jews and communists" reported there in 1941.
ST. GEORGEN	See MAUTHAUSEN.
ST. MIECHELS-GESTEL (Holland)	In February, 1944, camp at "De RUWENBERG" was reported as "camp for hostages". Inmates said to be deported as labour for works projects. SS controlled.
ST. NAZAIRE (France)	Angers region, Loire Inferieure.
ST. PAUL D'EYJAUX (France, Haute Vienne)	In August, 1943: 150 "communists", 130 Gaullists, and 150 persons interned for "sedition" and other reasons were reported to be there.
ST. PAUL-les-EAUX (France, Haute Vienne)	May be the same as preceding camp. Not confirmed as a German or Vichy operated KL, but may be a detention camp of another type.
ST. PRIVAS (France, Ardeche)	Not confirmed as KL.
ST. QUENTIN (France, Aisne)	Laon Region.
ST. RENAN (France, Finisterre)	Reported in December, 1943 as KL for 40,000 civilians in case of Allied invasion.
ST. SULPICE-LA-POINTE (France, Tarn)	January 1944: "KL for civilians" reported as removed from this location. August 1943: approximately 500 inmates reported there; "Gaullists and communists etc.

SAJMISTE
(ZEMUN)

See BELGRADE.

SALONIKA
(Greece)

1. **PAVLOS MELSS KL**
Macedonia: reported with 1,100 inmates in April 1944 and with 1,400 inmates in May, 1944. An undated report speaks of 700 inmates.

2. **SKOLIS KL**
Macedonia. 102 Sofia Street, SALONIKA.
Reported there with 400 inmates in April 1944.

SAMOS
(Greece, Island of Samos)

Unconfirmed report of KL.

SAPIEZYSKA
(Poland)

Near VILNA: reported in February, 1943 as a "punitive camp for forced labour". The name was also reported as SAPIERZYSKA.

SARVAR
(Yugoslavia)

A KL was reported there.

SCHAERBAKE
(Belgium)

Suburb of BRUSSELS.
Polizeigefängnis (?): see also JABBEKE.
SS Units in the Vicinity
Ersatzkommando der Waffen-SS (BRUSSELS)

SCHEVENINGEN
(Holland)

There are said to be 1,300 prisoners in SCHEVENINGEN, in the following two camps:-

1. The Oranje Hotel.
750 - 800 "political prisoners" reported to be interned there for interrogation by Sipo and Gestapo.

2. Police prison Nr. 850 on van Alkemade Laan.
Guards
German guards, SD and SS, who are subordinated to SD in DEN HAAG, Plein 1.
Personalities
Prison is commanded by Oschaf SCHWEIGER.
Prison Doctor is Dr. WERTENTERP, NSB who is also doctor for prisons on the Pompstations Road.

SCHIEDAM (Zuid Holland) Concentration Camp for women reported there.

SCHIRMITZ (Bayern) Near WEIDEN. Last reported in September, 1942.

SCHIRMECK (France, Haute Rhin) Alsace.

Type
Also called Sicherungslager VORBRÜCK bei SCHIRMECK. See also NATZWEILER.

Originally a transit camp of the French Army, it became a KL immediately following the French campaign.

Reported composed of 4 sections:
1. Police barracks
2. "Normal section" for inmates
3. Special section for inmates receiving especially harsh treatment
4. Women's section.

Inmates
July, 1941: 350 inmates.
September, 1941: 800.
January, 1942: 1,000. (The camp was still growing at the time.)
July, 1942: camp enlarged. 1,000-2,000.

"Volunteers for the Spanish war on the Loyalist side, homosexuals, priests, 'Grenzgänger' (smugglers and deserters) and political offenders" reported as inmates.

1944. Parents and entire families of Alsatians who deserted or attempted desertion from the German Army were interned there.

Identification
Prisoners are said to wear the following bands for identification:

Red cloth (4 x 5 cm)	Political
Red band around cap	Spanish war volunteers
Rectangle with small blue and brown squares	Social reasons
Green band around cap	Frontier jumpers
Blue band	Perverts
Blue cloth rectangle	Priests

SS Units in the Vicinity
SS Truppen Übungs Platz is near this camp.
SS Panzer Ersatz Abteilung (in BITSCH)
Bauleitung der Waffen-SS.

SCHIRMECK (contd.)	**Personalities**
	Camp Commandant is OSF BOUCK who was also reported as "Hauptmann der Sipo".
	A Schupo Lt. in charge of the guards (40 men).
	Three Zugwachtmeister, who work directly under his command.
SCHNEIDEMÜHL (Brandenburg)	Near Deutsch Krone. Last reported in 1936.
SCHOORL (North Holland)	KL.
SCHRÖTTERSBURG (PLOCK) (Poland)	KL probably identical with DOBRZYN. **SS Units in the Vicinity** SS Kraftfahrzeugamt der Waffen-SS. SS Kraftfahrschule III.
SCHUNEKER (France, Bas Rhin)	Alsace.
SCHWECHAT	See WIEN-SCHWECHAT.
SCHWETZ (SWIECIE) (NW Poland)	25 Km. ESE of GRAUDENZ. Reported in November, 1942, as KL for "Polish girls".
SEINES (N. Norway)	Reported as KL.
SEM (Norway)	Near TØNSBERG. For Jews.
SENFTENBERG (Brandenburg)	Near CALAU. Last reported 1936.
SENNELAGER (Westfalen)	Near PADERBORN. Last reported May, 1938. Possibly for military offenders from the Truppenübungsplatz there.
SENNHEIM (France, Alsace)	No details available. SS-Ausbildungslager in the area.
SETESDAL (S Norway)	No details.
SICHELBERG (SIERPC) (Poland)	112 Km. NW of WARSCHAU. Reported as KL.

SIEGBURG (Rheinland)	25 Km. SE of KÖLN. Reported as Arbeitslager, probably former Zuchthaus. Reported May 1938. In 1943 black marketeers were reported there.
SIERPC	See SICHELBERG.
SINGEN (Baden)	Near Asch. Camp reported there in November, 1942 for "prisoners and Germans from abroad"
SISTERON (France, Alpes Basses)	Marseilles region. 430 black market offenders and former police and camp officials.
SKALBMIERZ (Poland)	Reported as KL.
SKARZYSKO (Central Poland)	Near RADOM. June, 1943: reported as two "punitive camps for forced labour". October, 1943: reported as camp of the same type for Jews.
SKOLIS	See SALONIKA.
SLUIS (Holland)	Reported as a concentration camp for fascists before the invasion.
SMUKLA (SMUKALA) (Poland)	N. of BROMBERG. November, 1943: reported as "KL for children". January, 1944: reported as including adults.
SOBIEBOR (E.Poland)	65 Km. ENE of LUBLIN. Reported in September 1942 as KL and extermination camp for Jews.

SOLDAU (DZIALDOWO) (Ostpreussen)	65 Km. SSW of ALLENSTEIN.
	3 camps reported there:-
	   I Transit camp
	   II KL
	   III KL with special enclosures for women

SOLDIN (Brandenburg)	Definitely established in 1936. Last reported in March, 1938.

SOLEC
(Central Poland)

Near ILZA.
February, 1943: reported as "punitive camp for forced labour for Polish youths".

SOMOVIT
(Greece)

KL reported there.

SONNENBURG
(Brandenburg)

11 Km. E of KÜSTRIN.
Enlarged Zuchthaus turned into KL after 1933.
Inmates
    1933: 1,226 inmates were reported there.
    1936: 1,500 inmates reported there. 900 Norwegians.

Last reported in December, 1943.

SOSNOWIEC
(Poland)

5 Km. E of WARSCHAU, but may refer to SOSNOWICE (SOSNOWITZ) near KATTOWITZ, Oberschlesien.
Type
    Camp I. July, 1943: reported as transit and forced labour camp.
    Camp II. January, 1944: reported as KL.

SPIELBERG
(Mähren)

May not be a KL but a camp of another type.

STADELHEIM
(Bayern)

Near MÜNCHEN. Concentration camp last reported there in 1936.
SS Units in MÜNCHEN.
    SS Art. Ausbildungs- und Ersatz Regt.
    SS Flak Ersatz Regt. (SS Kaserne FREIMANN)
    SS Hauptreitschule (MÜNCHEN-RIEM)
    Berufsschule der Waffen-SS (SCHLEISSHEIM)
    SS Standortbereich
    SS Hauptfürsorge und Versorgungsamt (MÜNCHEN 27, Möhlstr. 12A)
    SS und Polizei Gericht
    Ergänzungsstelle der Waffen-SS (MÜNCHEN 27, Pienzenanerstr. 15)
    SS Lebensborn (Herzog Max Str. 3 - 7)
    SS Pferdezucht (MÜNCHEN - RIEM)

STARA GRADISKA
(STARE GRADISTE)
(Yugoslavia)

Croatia. KL under Ustashi control reported there.

STARACHOWICE
(Central Poland)

40 Km. NE KIELCE.
Reported once as KL, but in February, 1943 as "punitive camp for forced labour".

STAROGRAD	See PREUSSISCH STARGARD.
STAVERN (Norway)	Near LERVIK. Provisional KL for "students" reported in December, 1943. Said to have been previously a Russian PW camp. As 300 students are said to have been deported to Germany since above date, this camp may no longer be in operation.
STEPANOV (Czechoslovakia)	7 Km. SE of PRAG.
STETTIN (Pommern)	Located at the VULKAN WERFT (famous ship-building yards). Reported in operation in 1935. Took over part of camp HOHENBRÜCK in 1938. Was probably an independent camp, at least for a time, and reported as such in 1937. **Type** The camp was not a KL and has allegedly been disbanded. **Inmates** In 1940/41 a former inmate estimated there were 100 - 120 inmates "political and former Wehrmacht members". **Guard** 140 SS guards (reported by former inmate). **SS Units in the Vicinity** SS Sanitats Ersatz Bn. I. SS und Polizei Gericht Ergänzungsstelle der Waffen-SS (Friedrich Karlstrasse 3.). **Personalities** Dr. HOFFMANN said to be commandant at the time.
STRASSBURG (Alsace-Lorraine)	Yugoslav political prisoners.
STRELITZ (Mecklenburg)	Near FÜRSTENBERG. Last reported in February, 1941.
STUTTHOF (Danzig)	**Location** Near DANZIG. **Type** Official designation: Zivilgefangenlager. 1939-41: reported as KL for "Polish Priests and Civilians". November 1943: other nationalities such as Danes reported there.

STUTTHOF (contd.)

January 1944: Norwegians reported there.
SS operated.

SS Units in the Vicinity
SS Bereitschaften, the SS-Heimwehr DANZIG or elements of these units stationed near the camp.
Several companies of SS division "Galizien" held manoeuvres in this region. See DANZIG.

Personalities
SBF Paul Werner HOPPE of Waffen-SS reported to have assumed command.

SVANWIK
(Norway)

In Finnmark.

SVETA ANESTASIA
(Bulgaria)

Island near BURGAS. Reported to have 2,000 inmates and believed to be in operation.

SWATOBORSCHITZ, KYJOV
(SVATOBORICE)
(Böhmen-Mähren)

Both locations are given and camp may be near both places, which are probably between IGLAU and BRUENN.

Type
Internment Camp for relatives of refugees who are working outside Czechoslovakia.

Guards
Provided by the Gendarmerie of the Protectorate, while the Gestapo takes care of the trials.

Personalities
C.O. is the former 1st. Lt. of Gendarmerie CISAR, who now calls himself KAISER.

SWIECIE

See SCHWETZ.

SWIENTOCHLOWITZ
(SWIETOCHLOWICE)
(W Poland)

Reported as "punitive camp for forced labour".

SWIETY KRZYZ
(Central Poland)

October, 1943: reported as KL and labour camp for Jews.
Inmates estimated at 1,000.

SYLT

See ALDERNEY.

SYDSPISSEN
(Norway)

Near TROMSØ.

A103

SYNGROU
    (Greece)
Reported as prison but may well be a KL.

SZARVAS
    (Hungary)
For "peasants engaged in anti-war activities".

SZEBUNIA
    (Poland)
Jaslo County.   KL permanent camp.

T

TARNOW
(SW Poland) — Reported as KL and transit camp.

TARNOW II
(Poland) — Permanent KL

TARNOW III
(Poland) — KL with enclosure for women.

TATOI (TATOY)
(Greece)

Location
    Athens Area
Type
    KL reported
Inmates
    April 1944:   274
    June 1944 :   100
    July 1944:   851

TCZEW
(Poland) — Forced Labour Camp.

TEREZIN — See THERESIENSTADT

TERVUEREN
(Belgium) — Near BRUSSELS

THEBES (THIVE)
(Greece)

Attika Boeotia.
Type
    KL established by Italians in the town school.
Inmates
    October 1942:   600
    January 1943:   1,500
    February 1944:   92
    June   1944:   70
    July   1944:   116
    Undated report says 3,000 inmates.

THERESIENSTADT
(TEREZIN)
(Czechoslovakia) — Reported as extermination camp for Jews.
    Younger inmates are being transferred to the Government General.

THIVE — See THEBES.

THORN or TORUN
(NW Poland)   January 1943. Reported as
consisting of two camps:
KL I at PRININGHAUS (?) STEFANOWICZ.
KL II "SZMALCOWNIA".

TITHOREA
(Greece)   Phthiotis Phokis. KL reported
in June 1944, with 300 inmates.

TOLKEMIT
(Ostpreussen)   76 Km. SW of KONIGSBERG. Possibly
identical with BRAUNSBERG.

TOMASZOW
(Central Poland)   June 1943; reported as "punitive
camp for forced Labour".

TORGAU
(Halle-Merseburg)   Near DESSAU. Army Prison. 900
German soldiers reported here on
May 18th 1943.

TORUN   See THORN.

TOULOUSE
(France)   January 1944: sports ground
being fixed up for KL.
   See also RECEBEDOU for St.
Michel jail.

TRAWNIKI
(Poland)   Location
   Near CHELM in the LUBLIN
district.
Type
   July 1942: reported as
consisting of 3 camps:
I "punitive camp for forced
labour.
II KL for Jews. Inmates estimated
at 8,000.
III 30 Km. SE of LUBLIN.
Annihilation Camp.

TREBLINKA
(Poland)   Location
   80 Km. NE of WARSCHAU
Type
   September 1941: reported as
consisting of 3 camps.:
I "punitive camp for forced labour.
II KL
III Extermination camp for Jews.

TRESKAU   See POSEN-TRESKAU

TRIKKALA
    (Greece)   Thessaly. Reported as KL

TRIPOLIS
    (Greece)   Peloponnese. KL established
                                by Italians.

TROPPAU
    (OPAWA)   May also be OPPAWA (OPPAU).
                                Confirmed in 1939.
                                October 1943: reported as transit
                                camp for "expropriated people".

TRUTZDORF.   See WÖLLERSDORF-TRUTZDORF.

TSCHENSTOCHAU or
CZESTOCHOWA   Location
                                    60 Km. N of KATTOWITZ.
                                Type
                                    Reported as "punitive camp for
                                forced labour".
                                    Six further camps planned.
                                Inmates
                                    Estimated 600 - 1,000.
                                Remarks
                                    There is a ghetto in this town
                                and the latter may have been reported
                                in error as a KL.

TSIKALA
    (Greece)   Thessaly.

TUEDESTRAND
    (Norway)   No details.

U

ULVEN (Norway)

Location
 Near Bergen. Former Exerzierplatz.
 ULVEN said to have been abandoned after ESPELUND was enlarged.

Inmates
 January 1944: 100 - 200 inmates reported there, all of them from the Bergen area.
 Inmates work mostly on jobs outside the camp.

Guards
 German Police.

UCKERMARK (Brandenburg)

Location
 Post FÜRSTENBERG, Mecklenburg. Possibly identical with with RAVENSBRÜCK.

Type
 Reported in May 1944 as Jugendschutzlager der Sipo for girls.

UNTERMASSFELD (Thüringen)

Near Meiningen. Reported May 1938. Not confirmed.

UTRECHT (Holland)

House of Detention (GANSSTRAAT). Possibly not KL.

V

VALKENBURG
(Holland)   KL

VAL-LES-BAINS
(France)

Ardeche (Lyons Region)
Political internees.

VANNES
(France, Morbihan)

Type
   Not confirmed as German or Vichy operated KL.
   May be a detention camp of another type.
Inmates
   Reported to have 2,000. British civilians also said to be detained there.

VARNA
(Bulgaria)

2,000 inmates reported there. Believed to be in operation.

VECHTA
(Oldenburg)

Confirmed until May 1938.

VEEHUTZEN
(Holland)

May be identical with WESTERBORK. 900 Jews reported there, June 1943.

VELIKA-KANIJA
(Yugoslavia)

KL reported there.

VERDALSOREN
(Norway)

Near TRONDHJEM; reported as camp for "German deserters".

VESOUL
(France Haute-Saone)

Reported in May 1943 as PW camp, and in January 1944 as KL with 4,141 French inmates.

VICHY
(France, Alliers)

No camp there, but according to a report from December 1943, "several camps were planned in case of an Allied invasion".

1. At the CONCOURS HIPPIQUE near the Sichon River and railway.
2. At the STADIUM near the confluence of the Sichon and Allier rivers.

    3. At the race tracks on the left bank of the Allier river opposite footbridge.
    4. Covering a part of the airfield N of Vichy on the right bank of the Allier river near RHUE.

VIDAUBAN.
    (France, Var)　　Reported in August 1942, as "camp for aliens"; not confirmed as KL.

VILIAMPOLE
    (Lithuania)　　Suburb of KAUNAS.

VILNA　　See WILNO

VINCENNES
    (France, Seine)　　According to a report of November 1943, the CHATEAU DE VINCENNES is "a centre of persecution and torture".

VOLOS
    (Greece).　　Thessaly; KL situated near railway station, and reported with 350 hostages, June 1944.

VORBRUCK　　See SCHIRMECK

VOULGIAMENI
    (Greece)　　9 miles E of PIREAUS; unconfirmed report of KL there.

VOVES
    (France, Eure-et-Loire)　　Reported in June, 1943, as camp for political internees; said to hold 850 Communists and socialists.

VUGHT.
    (Holland)

Type
    KL. Known as KL LOWER HERTOGENBOSCH
    A gas chamber us under construction there.

Capacity
    7,000.
    Camp was to be enlarged to over 20,000 in March, 1943.

Inmates
    March, 1943: 4 - 5,000 reported there.
    August 1943: report claimed 1,800 - 2,500 inmates.
    January 1944: 4,500 Dutchmen, and many Belgians, French and other Europeans reported there.

All Jews in Holland have to report there.

It is said that the Dutch Communists have a strong position in the internal camp management. For instance Jan HURKMANS, the Lagerälteste and right hand man of the commandant, is said to belong to them.

Identifications

Reichsdeutsche are recognizable by a green patch.

Dutch political prisoners who are members of the Dutch Communist Party wear a red triangle.

SS Units in the Vicinity

An SS Truppen Übungs Platz is located near the camp.

Elements of SS Polizei Regiment 1 (motorisiert).

Other SS Polizei Regiment elements.

Personalities

Commander was arrested in the middle of January 1944 on account of "scandalous conduct".

The camp doctor is Dr. WOLTER, an SS man with previous KL experience.

Other Camps.

There are two outside camps, probably branches of this one:
  GILZE FLJEN
  KOERDIJK (about 400 inmates)

VULKAN WERFT — See STETTIN

VURIA (?) PIRAEUS
(Greece)

Athens area: established by Germans.
KL reported in June 1943, with 81 hostages from Crete.
Used as transit camp.

WALDENBURG
  (Schlesien)   S of Breslau. Last reported in
                        May 1938

WANNE-EICKEL
  (Westfalen)   Reported in May 1938, and believed
                        to be an administrative centre.

WARSCHAU (WARSZAWA)
  (Poland)   1. **Camp at Skaryszewa Street.**
                        Reported in November 1942 as a
                        transit camp for "forced labour"
                        with approximately 7,000 inmates.

                        2. **Camp at Gesia Street.**
                        Reported in July 1943 as KL and in
                        October 1943, as "punitive camp for
                        forced labour" especially for Polish
                        Youth.
                        Units in the vicinity.
                            SS Polizei Rgt. 22
                            SS Kavalerie Ersatz Bat.
                               Elements of Totenkopf Standarte
                               Obb.(?)
                            SS Panzer Grenadier Ausbildungs
                               und Ersatz Bn. 3.
                            SS Radfahrer Ausbildungs und
                               Ersatz Unit.
                            SS Unterführer Schule.
                               Bekleidungslager der Waffen SS
                            SS Hauptveterinärpark
                               Kurierstelle der Waffen SS.

WASSERBURG/Inn
  (Bayern)   Believed to be in operation.

WATENSTEDT   See EMSLAND (Location of Göring Works)

WATTEN
  (France, Nord)   **Type**
                            September 1943: a camp for
                        "political internees" was reported
                        here.
                        Remarks
                            "Undesirables are said to wear
                        yellow stripes and "bandits" green
                        stripes on their trousers.

WATTENSCHEID
  (Westfalen)   Near BOCHUM: last reported as a KL
                        in 1936.

WAUER
  (Poland)   Dulag reported near AUSCHWITZ in 1940.

WEIMAR
  (Thüringen)

Type
There is an internment camp at FORST ETTERSBURG, with 75 buildings and a factory, according to a report dated September 1943.
Remarks
BUCHENWALD is at times referred to as WEIMAR.

WELZHEIM
  (Würtemberg)

Near Schorndorf.   Last reported in April 1937.

WESTERBORK
  (Holland)

Type
Large KL for Jews reported there in June 1943.
May be identical with VEENHUIZEN.
Remarks
2200 prisoners, many ill, were transported in cattle cars from camp Westerbork on July 20th, 1943.

WETZLAR
  (Nassau)

Reported before 1939; not confirmed.

WIELRENIA

See KIELCE.

WIEN-SCHWECHAT
  (Reg. Bez. Wien)

South of Vienna.   Concentration camp reported there.
SS Units in the Vicinity
SS Kraftfahrausb. und Ers. Komp)
  Kraftfahrtechn. Lehranstalt   )
  der Waffen SS   )
SS Bauschule
SS Ingenieurschule, WIEN IX,
      Wälringerstr. 67
  Hauptwirtschaftslager der Waffen SS.
SS Standortkommandantur.
  Ergähzungsstelle der Waffen SS
  (Wien IX/66, Lichtensteinstr. 49
  Ers. Inspektion der Waffen SS,
      SÜDOSTRAUM.)
      (Wien XIII, Gloriettegasse
                        14 - 16)
SS und Polizeigericht
SS Feldpostprüfung Zweigstelle SÜDOST.
  (Wien VII, Mariahilfestr. 38 - 48).
SS Passierscheinzweigstelle (Wien IX,
  Seegasse 9)
SS Lazarett
SS Röntgensturmbann (Grosse Stadtgutgasse 28)

WIERDEN-ALMELO
(Holland)
KL reported as WIERDEN I and II near ALMELO.

WILGA
(Central Poland)
Near GARWOLIN.
Type
Reported in July, 1942, as KL for Jews and "punitive camp for forced labour".

WILNO (VILNA)
(East Poland)
Type
Reported in October, 1943, as "punitive camp for forced labour" Said to be located at DOBRA RADA STREET)

WILSEDE
(Hessen-Nassau)
S of Lüneburg
Last reported in May 1938.

WINNICA
(Poland)
12 Km SW of Pultusk. Transit camp.

WITTLICH
See KALKTURM

WITTMOOR
See HAMBURG

WLOCLAWEK
See LESLAU

WOLLERSDORF-TRUTZDORF
(Niederdonau)
Under DOLLFUSS and SCHUSCHNIGG mainly Nazi inmates; therefore renamed TRUTZDORF.
Several barracks burned down in 1938 and closed.
Said to be again in operation.

WOLFENBÜTTEL
(Braunschweig)
Identified in 1943.

WRONKI
(W Poland)
Probably called WRONKEN by the Germans.
Reported as "punitive camp for forced labour".
Reported to be an old prison.

WUPPERTAL
(Rheinland)

At Wuppertal. Camp last reported there in January 1944 had 1,800 prisoners.

WÜRZBURG
(Bayern)

A camp was last reported there in 1936.

WYSOKIE BRZEGI
(W Poland)

Near JEZORA. A town named WYSOKIE has been renamed HOHENAU. Reported as "punitive camp for forced labour".

XANTHI
    (Greece)　　　　　　　　　Western Thrace; KL established
    　　　　　　　　　　　　by Bulgarians; capacity unknown.

Y

YERYERI (AMARIOU) RETHYMNOS
    (Greece)　　　　　　　　　Crete; reported as KL

YPATI
    (Greece)　　　　　　　　　KL reported with 90 inmates in
    　　　　　　　　　　　　February 1944.

YVOIR
    (Belgium, Namur　　　　　A report of January 1942, states
    　　　　　Province)　　　　that a camp with barbed wire enclosures was under construction there; believed to be intended as KL.

Z

ZABIKOWO
    (S. Poland)　　　　　　　Near Poznan; a forced labour camp
    　　　　　　　　　　　　is reported there.

ZACISZE
    (Poland)　　　　　　　　Reported in November 1941 as a
    　　　　　　　　　　　　Straflager "for peasants."
    　　　　　　　　　　　　There are 3 towns by this name in
    　　　　　　　　　　　　Poland.

ZAGREB
(Yugoslavia)

Type
There is a concentration camp near the Zoo at MAXIMIE, near ZAGREB.

Remarks
Jews there wear, back and front, a yellow patch with David's Star and a "Z".
The SS Einsatzstaffel composed of Volksdeutsche used to kill Jews in the streets of Zagreb.

Personalities
Name of Gestapo under SBF is unknown but the man is reported to be a relative of Dr. UBERREITER Gauleiter STEIERMARK.

ZAKRZOWEK
(Central Poland)

Near ILZA; reported in February 1943, as "punitive labour camp".

ZAMARTE
(NW Poland)

Near KONITZ.
In January 1943, confirmed as KL

ZAMBROW
(NE Poland)

Reported in February 1943, as "punitive camp for forced labour".

ZAMOSK
(Central Poland)

Type
Reported in January 1943 as transit camp for "expropriated Poles"

SS units in the Vicinity
SS Pferdesammel- und Ersatzlager.
SS Reit-und Fahrschule.

ZANTI.
(Greece)

Macedonia. KL reported under Bulgarian control.

ZASCANKI
(Poland)

KL reported in November 1943

ZASCIENEK
(Poland)

Near BIALYSTOK; KL may be same as ZASCIANKI.

ZGIERZ

See GÖRNAU

ZICHENAU (CIECHANOW)
(Poland)

Location
78 Km NNW of WARSAW

Type
One permanent KL and three forced labour camps are reported in this district.

ZÖRBIG
(Sachsen)

Near MERSEBURG; reported May 1933.

ZWIERZYNIEC
(Central Poland)

Near LUBLIN.
Reported in October 1943, as "transit and punitive camp for forced labour".

ZWRINGEN
(Unlocated)

Believed to be in operation.

Unlocated Camps

KL between NEUSTADT and NEISSE in Schlesien; reported in August 1943.

SK Lager for suspected German soldiers returning from the Russian front was reported as having started in September 1942.

KL between LEIPZIG and BRESLAU, especially for Jews reported in March 1944.

KL for German officers and other ranks reported in Eastern Prussia in June 1943.
There are said to be 2,000 prisoners dressed in Polish uniforms in order to hide the fact that so many Germans had been "bad boys" at the Eastern Front.

A special KL for people having connections with England and the USA is said to have been set up in Southern Germany.
The report, dated April 1944, expresses the belief that Hitler will hold these people as hostages to protect himself.

ANNEXE A

Part III

List of SS Arbeitsstäbe not located Near an Identified Concentration Camp

BREST Kr. LESLAU, Gutsverwaltung, Popowiczki

ELSENAU, Kirchenstrasse 6

GEMLITZ Kr. MOGILNO, Dietfurt 22 Gumbitz

GNESEN, Gottestrasse 22

GOSTINGEN, Bahnhofstrasse 33

HIRSCHTEICH, Lützowstrasse 2 (SS Werkzentrale)

POTTKORST, Dietfurt, Gutsverwaltung Blüchersfelde

RAWITSCH, Breslauer Stadtgraben 13

SCHIERAK, Friedhofstrasse 6

SCHRIMM, Bahnhofstrasse 3

SCHRODA, Rigaer Strasse 5

STERNBRUCK, Kempen, Hirscheck

TUREK, Wolhynieneinsatz, Strasse des 13 Sept, 26

WARTHBRÜCKEN, Schachtahusstrasse 12

WEHLUNGEN, Krakauer Vorstadt 15

WOLLSTEIN, Eichengraben-Oberhof

WRESCHEN, Helmuth-Raymannstrasse 6

ZIRKE, Birnbaum, Markt 19

CONFIDENTIAL

SUPREME HEADQUARTERS ALLIED EXPEDITIONARY FORCE
EVALUATION AND DISSEMINATION SECTION
G-2 (COUNTER INTELLIGENCE SUB-DIVISION)

B-A-S-I-C H-A-N-D-B-O-O-K

KL's

(Konzentrationslager)

AXIS CONCENTRATION CAMPS AND DETENTION CENTRES

REPORTED AS SUCH IN EUROPE

ANNEXE B

Diagram

E.D.S./G/6
   Compiled by MIRS (LONDON Branch)
   From Material Available at
   WASHINGTON and LONDON.

Key to the KL Organisation Chart (See also text, para. 6)

1. This chart is a combination of facts and conjectures.

2. Kripo (Kriminalpolizei) and Gestapo are responsible for Einweisung (Committment to KL's). The Kripo deals with Berufsverbrecher (habitual criminals) and the Gestapo with all other Schutzhäftlinge (those in protective custody).

3. The Kommandantur (KL Administration office) is in control of:-

    Rationing
    Ordnance of Kdfr. personnel
    Post Office
    Censorship
    Clothing Store
    Bookkeeping, pay and accounts

4. The Lagerführer (Camp Sub. Commandant) controls:-

    Barracks
    SS Blockführer   (SS Block Leaders)
    +Stubenältester (Room wardens)
    +Lagerältester   (Senior inmates)
    SS-Arbeitsdienstführer (Works Supervisor)
    +Clerical Staff.

5. The Lazarett (hospital) Entwesung etc. controls:-

    SS Doctor
    Inmates Doctor
    +Nurses
    Inmates Hospital
    Disinfecting Station

+ Positions filled by inmates.

ANNEXE B

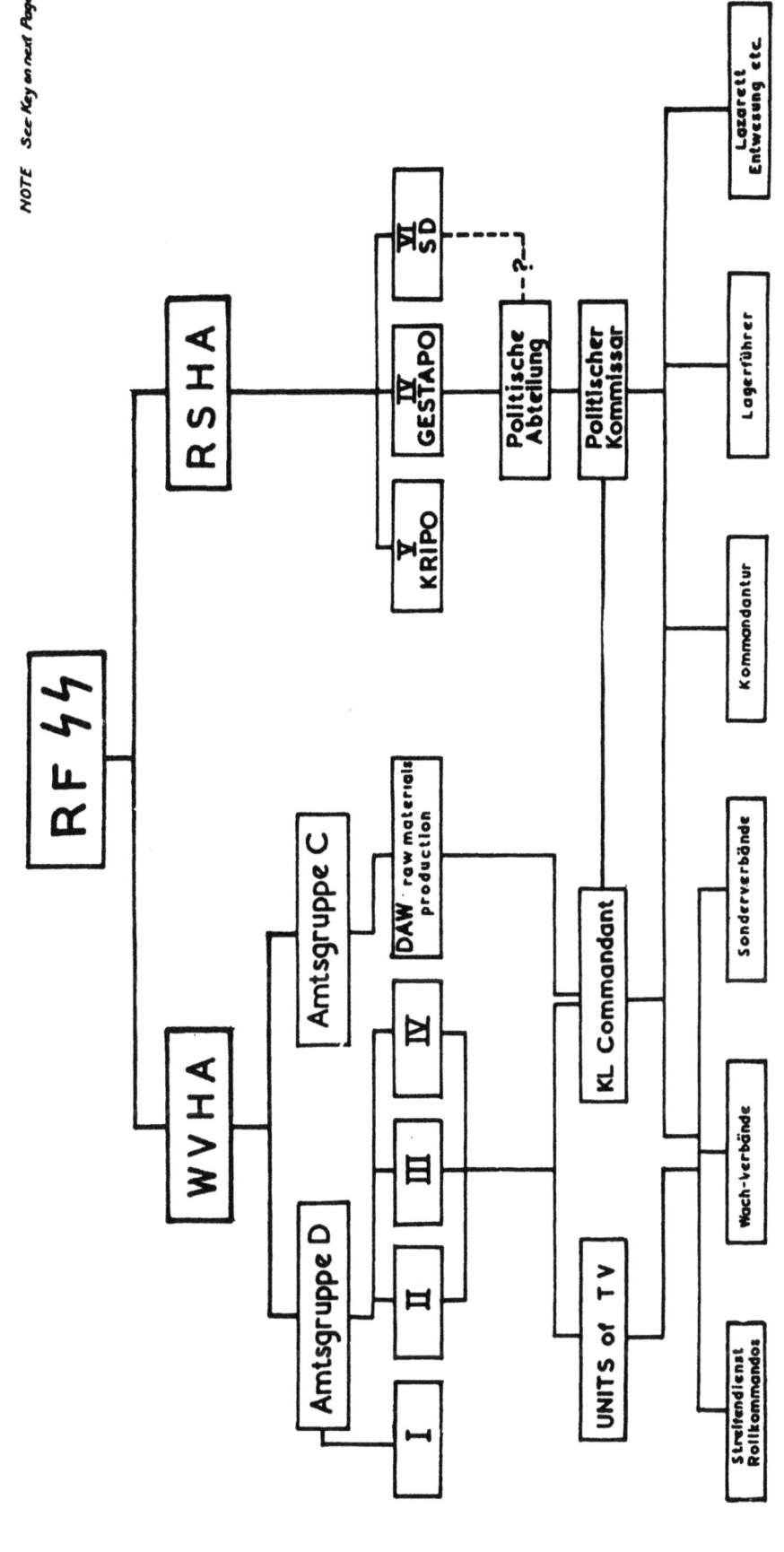

The War to end all Wars
The Great War 1914–1918

A vast selection of titles available at
www.naval-military-press.com

Books for the Battlefield Tourist
Divisional Histories
Eastern Front & the Balkans
Russian Civil War Intervention
Memoirs, Biographies and Diaries
Militaria, Uniforms, Headgear, and Weapons
Official Histories
Other Theatres
Reference Works

Regimental Histories of the British Army
Regimental Histories of the Empire
Rolls of Honour, Casualty lists and Genealogy
The War at Sea
The War in the Air
Training Manuals, Text books and Instructions
Western Front

www.ingramcontent.com/pod-product-compliance
Lightning Source LLC
Chambersburg PA
CBHW081544090426
42743CB00014BA/3129